PRAY
As You Can

PRAY
As You Can

Discovering Your Own Prayer Ways

Jean Gill

AVE MARIA PRESS
NOTRE DAME, INDIANA 46556

© 1989 by Ave Maria Press, Notre Dame, Indiana 46556
All rights reserved. No part of this book may be used or
reproduced in any manner whatsoever without written
permission, except in the case of reprints in the context of reviews.

International Standard Book Number: 0-87793-403-7
0-87793-402-9 (pbk.)

Library of Congress Catalog Card Number: 89-83991

Cover Design: Katherine Robinson Coleman

Printed and bound in the United States of America

Dedication
to Walt
whose love and trust
inspires and encourages me

CONTENTS

ACKNOWLEDGMENTS

I am grateful to my family, friends and fellow travelers, who have affirmed and encouraged me all along my journey.

Special thanks are due to those for whom I have been privileged to be spiritual companion and director. They have entrusted to me their stories of the unique and special ways in which God has touched them. I am particularly grateful to those who have permitted me to include their stories in *Pray As You Can* with names and details changed in order to protect the confidentiality in which they shared their experiences with me.

I am especially grateful to those who reviewed the manuscript and shared with me their valuable suggestions and comments: Tee Gardner; J. Ripley Caldwell, S.J.; Jorge daSilva, S.M.; my sister Sharon Lippard; Marie Langenes. I owe particular thanks to Bill Langenes for his help in producing the manuscript in its final form.

My deep appreciation goes to my husband, Walt, for his love, his enthusiastic support and his valuable suggestions.

INTRODUCTION

Trust your Self.
Trust your Self to explore . . . to discover . . .
    and to rediscover . . . your own unique ways to pray
        those special pathways that you follow
            as you travel along your spiritual journey . . .
        your own route . . .
            similar to the ways that others have
                traveled . . .
                    yet different from any of the others . . .
        the route whose direction is revealed to you
            by the Spirit of God . . .
        the Spirit of Love and Life
            who beckons you to come ever closer . . .
        to feel the fire of God's love
            and the power of God's life . . .
        to be consumed by that Love and that Life,
            to be one with God . . .
        and in God, to become ever more fully and deeply
            the unique and special person
                your loving Creator calls you to be . . .
        and to be thus enabled to share
            God's abundant life and love
                with those whose lives you touch.

The spiritual journey can be confusing at times. Sometimes we come to a fork in the road and we don't know
which way to turn. We are afraid to make a mistake, afraid
we will be sidetracked from our destination. Sometimes our
destination is not clear. We may not be sure whether the
Spirit of God or some deceptive or evil spirit is leading us.
Yet we each have a trustworthy guide: our unconscious inner
Self, a seemingly unlimited source of wisdom, strength, creativity, courage, goodness and healing power. Our inner
Self is a powerful resource for us as we try to choose the
paths that lead to fullness of life, the ways that bring us
closer to the Spirit of Life.

In contrast with our unconscious Self, let us consider
the role of our conscious ego-self in the spiritual journey.
Our ego-self is that extremely valuable and important ability
whereby we think and choose and control our lives. *Ego* is
the Latin word for *I*. The ego-self is "I, myself." We refer to
this self when we say, "I, myself, think, choose or do this."

Our ego-self is limited to whatever has been incorporated into our conscious awareness. Wherever the word *self*
is used in this book, it means the conscious ego-self. The
unconscious Self will be designated by a capital letter. This
use of small and large type suggests the relatively small and
limited scope of our ego-self in contrast with the larger,
apparently unlimited resources of our unconscious Self.

Our ego-self must be reasonably strong and confident,
for we need to make frequent and courageous choices if we
are to persevere on the spiritual journey. One particularly
critical choice we need to make repeatedly along the journey
is the decision to let go of the illusions and preconceived
notions of our ego-self, what *I* think reality is like or should
be like. It means letting go of our conscious perceptions and
letting our unconscious Self lead us to new ways of seeing
and acting and being.

One common roadblock for most of us on the spiritual
journey involves the very notion of prayer itself. We each
have our own idea of what is meant by prayer, and our idea

of what it is or should be tends to limit our choice of prayer ways. One of the wisest and most practical bits of traditional advice about prayer is: "Pray as you can, not as you can't." When we pray the way we or others think we *should* pray, we are very likely to be praying "as we can't," rather than the way we can and will pray.

We see an illustration of this roadblock on the journey in the experience of a woman who came to me for spiritual direction. She told me of the difficulties she was having trying to pray in her usual way—the way she had been taught. She felt guilty that prayer seemed a chore and that she did not feel in touch with God. Prayer was not fruitful or nourishing for her. She felt she must be doing something wrong. We talked about other ways she might pray, and she decided that drawing pictures of her feelings and experiences was something she would like to try. She brought several pictures to our next meeting. Each one expressed in a very vibrant way the movement of the Spirit in her life. She felt very much in touch with God, and her time spent in prayer had become life-giving, interesting and challenging—the way we would expect our time spent with a good friend to be! She said, shaking her head in wonderment, "I just never would have thought that drawing pictures could be prayer!"

When we set limits on our concept of prayer we limit our concept of God in the process. God is infinite and can enter into our lives in an infinite variety of ways. When we restrict the ways we will pray, we restrict the ways we will allow God to touch us. Our ego-self needs to let go of preconceived notions of prayer and let our inner Self suggest new ways to touch and be touched by God.

When we pray in ways that help our ego-self to be in touch with our unconscious inner Self, we are closer to the Spirit within. We read in the story of creation that we are made in the image and likeness of God (Gn 1:26-27). The more truly we come to know our Self, the more clearly we see God reflected in our own image.

We read in Paul's letter to the Corinthians: "Now we see indistinctly, as in a mirror; then we shall see face to face" (1 Cor 13:12). Our inner Self gives us a much clearer, truer image of who we are than our conscious ego-self. From the viewpoint of our ego-self, the image of our true Self is clouded and indistinct. We see ourselves the way we think we should be, rather than the way we really are. Likewise, we see God the way we think God should be rather than the way God truly is. When we look more deeply and perceive our inner Self, it is as if several layers of dark film were wiped from the mirror, and we are able to see a truer image of our Self reflected there. We see the true image of God reflected more clearly in this image of our Self. It is as if we catch a momentary glimpse of God "face to face." We experience an intimate moment with God.

The song "Only a Shadow"* by Carey Landry beautifully and poignantly expresses this sense of the intimate connection between our Self image and the image of God:

> The love I have for You, my Lord,
>> is only a shadow of Your love for me,
>> . . . Your deep abiding love.
> My own belief in You, my Lord,
>> is only a shadow of Your faith in me,
>> . . . Your deep and lasting faith. . . .
> The dream I have today, my Lord,
>> is only a shadow of Your dreams for me;
>> only a shadow of all that will be
>>> if I but follow You.
> The joy I feel today, my Lord,
>> is only a shadow of Your joys for me
>> . . . when we meet face to face.

---

* "Only A Shadow" by Carey Landry Copyright ©1971 is from the collection *Hi God!* available from NALR, 10802 N. 23rd Ave., Phoenix, AZ 85029 in cassette and accompaniment.

The more clearly we see our true Self the more clearly we see God. The more in touch we are with our Self, the more in touch we are with God. The more "Self centered" our prayer is, the more "God centered" it is!

It is important to distinguish Self centered from ego-self centered prayer. In ego-self centered prayer we are too controlling; we inhibit the deeper movements of the Spirit from within. In Self centered prayer, we are open to the Spirit praying and moving within us. For instance, we can pray with scripture in a Self centered way in which we watch and wait. *We allow our self to be moved from within by the word.* We can also pray with scripture in an ego-self centered way in which, perhaps, we may consciously try to see how the passage applies to our life. *We try to move the word into the place we think it should fit.*

The difference between the two ways of prayer is like the difference between a sip of water and an unlimited ocean. The ego-self centered way is like drinking a small sip of God, where we carefully measure and control how much we will be touched by God. The Self centered way is like floating in the ocean of God, where we allow the Spirit of God to move us. All of us are surrounded by God; it is a matter of whether we choose to let go and float or to stand on the pier and let God affect us only in tiny drops.

As we discover our own unique pathways of prayer that lead us to our deeper Self, we can draw closer to God in an ever more intimate relationship. We can relate to God more honestly, more as we really are and less as we think we should be. We can let God be more the way God truly is, and less the way we think God is or should be. We can allow the Spirit to reveal more clearly the most life-giving direction for us at any given place on our journey.

In this book we will consider Self centered ways of prayer—ways that help us to let go of our ego-self control and to be open to the movements of the Spirit from our

inner Self. We will look closely and deeply at the process
involved and explore ways to discern the presence and
movement of the Spirit of God in the experience of prayer.
We will seek ways to grow in trusting our own perception
of the direction in which the Spirit is leading us.

Let us set out together on a journey of exploration,
    an adventure of discovery.
Let us trust our Self
    to find our own unique ways
        to walk with God on our journey.
Let us trust our Self
    to learn to dance along the path . . .
        our own special dance in rhythm with the Spirit
            of God . . .
    to be able to change and grow
        and learn new steps in our dance with the
            Spirit . . .
    to find new directions in our path.
Let us trust our Self
    to be able to follow the Spirit with confidence . . .
        the Spirit of Life and Love . . .
            who longs to lead each of us to abundant life
               and love and happiness.
Let us trust God in the depths of our Self . . .
    and believe that our own deep desire for God
        is "only a shadow"
            of God's passionate desire for us.
Let us believe that we only need to let go . . .
    and to be open to God
        in whatever tiny ways we are able . . .
    and that God will respond with eagerness . . .
        illuminating our path . . .
    and then running exuberantly to meet us
        with arms flung wide
            to embrace each of us
               in divine and fervent love.

ONE

House of Many Windows

Prayer is like a window. It is our way of opening our self to God. It is the response to our deep desire to allow the Spirit of God to blow through our souls, to feel the movement of God within our Self, to hear the whisper or the roar or the music of God's voice; to look and see the image of God imprinted within our Self; to allow God's hand to reach deep within our hearts to touch us and to mold us; to breathe deeply of God's Spirit; to be filled with God to the height and the depth and the breadth of our being.

Each of us is like a house with many windows. The house, our ego-self, is the place we know, the place where we feel comfortable. The windows, our prayer ways, open out to our limitless Self, where the Spirit of God moves freely, blowing this way or that, always there and ready to blow into our conscious self to touch and to move us, to disturb us, to caress and to comfort us.

The windows vary in shape, size and style. They open

in different ways. We open some of the windows often and
easily: our preferred ways of prayer. Other windows we may
seldom or never open: ways of prayer that are difficult, un-
attractive or unknown to us. Some of the windows, in the
basement or the attic, are perhaps dusty and stiff from in-
frequent use. Yet these attic and basement windows can be
very special. Through them we may discover the heights
and depths of God's presence and action in our lives that we
have not yet experienced.

Consider the possible effects of limiting our self to any
particular way or ways of prayer. Suppose, for instance, that
we are accustomed to setting aside a certain period of time
to spend with the Lord in prayer. During this time we
normally pray with a scripture passage, or talk with God
about our present life experiences, or pray for other people,
or spend the time simply being still in God's presence. Perhaps we use a combination, but we have limited our self to
praying in these ways. We open a few prayer-windows in
that part of our house where we are most comfortable. For
a time, we are satisfied with our prayer. It seems nourishing
and we feel in touch with God.

Then something may change. Our prayer may seem
boring or dry, we may feel distant from God, perhaps distractions disturb us more frequently. Our prayer no longer
seems as satisfying or nourishing as before. The flow of our
prayer seems to be blocked. The barrier can be the very
way we have chosen to pray. We can become so accustomed
to certain ways of prayer that unconsciously we limit our
interaction with God to those ways. Our prayer becomes
ego-self centered and controlled, rather than Self centered
and open.

We may still seek the Lord in prayer through our usual
windows, not realizing that the wind has shifted and the
Spirit is calling us to open a new window. We may need to
go to a different part of the house, to a window we have not
opened before now. Perhaps we have tried to open it and

it was too stiff, or we felt uncomfortable in that part of the house. Certain prayer-windows we simply have never considered opening. Perhaps we did not notice they were there, or it has not occurred to us that the Spirit could or would come in to us through them.

We have much in common with others, and so we can all use some basic ways of prayer more or less effectively. But we need to adapt these ways to our own individuality. Each of us is a unique and special person, and we need to find our own ways of prayer.

All houses have basic features such as doors and windows, rooms where we eat and sleep, and a roof overhead. But the unlimited variety in style and color and shape reflects our individuality. As we explore the ways of prayer that will be most effective for us, we each need to pay attention to the unique kind of house that we are. Windows need to harmonize with the style and shape of a house and be located at the best vantage point for proper light and ventilation. We may remodel the house of our ego-self from time to time, as we change and grow and discover more of our true and unique Self. Our prayer-windows will need to be remodeled also to correspond to the changes in ourselves.

My husband and I are currently involved in building a new home. We find that we continually draw on books and magazines, professional architects, interior designers and builders for ideas in designing, building and remodeling. From these resources, we need to decide what reflects our unique needs and tastes, what makes a house feel like home to us. Likewise, many resources for learning prayer such as books and magazines, spiritual directors and retreat leaders can offer us an opportunity to learn basic techniques and possible variations. Then we need to design our own unique ways of feeling at home with those prayer ways.

Another image might help us understand how we discover our own prayer ways. As we read a book or listen to a talk on prayer, we might approach it as we would a cook-

book. Scan it and notice what appeals to you. Then try out
a few prayer recipes. Try different types for a balanced diet.
See how each one tastes. We may find one that does not
taste good at all, so we may decide not to use it again. Since
our taste changes with time we may want to try it again
another time. Maybe another prayer recipe is tasty and
nourishing, but we will adjust the ingredients a bit the next
time we use it. Another way may suit us so well that we use
it frequently. We become bored with it in time and may
need to set it aside for a while or vary it in some way.

One excellent resource for prayer is *Sadhana: A Way
to God* by Anthony de Mello (The Institute of Jesuit Sources,
1978, and Image Books, 1984). *Sadhana* lends itself especially well to the cookbook approach, since the exercises are
divided into sections corresponding to three basic types of
prayer. We need to try prayer exercises from all three sections for a balanced diet of spiritual nourishment.

How can we discern which ways of prayer lead us toward God and which ways lead us away from God? We learn
to pray by praying. If we enter into the prayer journey with
the commitment to spend time regularly in prayer, we will
learn the terrain. We will learn by becoming lost and then
finding our way again. We will learn by feeling the road
under our feet and the wind in our face or at our back. In
this way we will also learn to trust our Self. As we experiment with various prayer ways, we might notice which enable us to become centered and lead us to contemplative
experience.

Two terms occur regularly in both traditional and con-
temporary literature on prayer: *centering* and *contemplation*. Both are desirable aspects of any form of prayer if they
are considered in the broad sense of their basic meaning
rather than as specific ways or stages of prayer.

Centering can mean simply having our attention focused. We need to pay attention in order to notice God
speaking to us. The more Self centered we are, the more
clearly we can hear God. Innumerable methods can focus

our attention, and we need to find the ways that work best for each of us. Some people center by noticing their breathing, by repeating a mantra or chant, by paying attention to body sensations or by using a simple, still image. Others need a more active way, such as entering imaginatively into a scripture story and letting it capture their attention. Still others focus their attention on a single object such as a rock or a flower, perhaps holding it in their hands.

Becoming centered involves learned skills. We may need to practice these techniques for a time, which calls for patience, discipline and commitment. Perhaps we might combine two contrasting centering methods during the learning process, in time discerning which is more effective. For example, ten minutes of a prayer period may be spent in focusing on body sensations, followed by ten minutes of active imagination with a scripture story, or vice versa. As we begin to see which method is more fruitful for us, we can adjust the proportion of time accordingly. We may find that one or the other method consistently works better for us, or we may find that it varies from one prayer period to another.

Contemplation flows out of centering. As we focus our attention, we may notice a shift or a movement such as the surfacing of a feeling, or a sense of deeper stillness, or an increase of intensity. To contemplate is to stop, to be still, to experience deeply whatever is presenting itself—to look, to touch, to feel, to hear the presence or movement of the Spirit within our Self as fully and deeply as possible at the moment. Contemplation is a quality or attitude that can be developed in any form of prayer.

An important characteristic of contemplation is that we let go of conscious, ego-self control and are open to newness and surprises from the Spirit within our Self. There is a childlike quality about it, an open, searching, exploring, adventurous attitude. It often calls for courage in the face of the unknown.

We need to be open and flexible as we experiment,

willing to follow the direction of the Spirit rather than our own plan. For example, suppose I have planned to spend some time praying with Psalm 139. I slowly begin to read, "O Lord, you have probed me and you know me." The word *probed* catches my attention. I become centered on the word. I pause. I notice a feeling of discomfort surfacing. I can go on and finish reading the psalm as I, myself, planned, or I can allow this moment to become contemplative. I can stop, be still, be open to my Self, and experience the feeling more deeply. I may need to overcome some resistance, since it is a disturbing feeling. It will take some courage to stay with it. My childlike inclination to search and be open to surprise can help to counteract my urge to move on.

We need to move slowly in prayer so that something can catch our attention. For example, if I were reading Psalm 139 at a normal pace, I may have read right through the word *probed* too quickly to allow my attention to be centered on it. Then the contemplative experience would not have had an opportunity to develop. We will look at more examples of centering and contemplation as we consider a variety of prayer ways in subsequent chapters.

TWO

Picture Windows
Imagination and Dreams

One of our most important prayer-windows is the picture window of our imagination. When we look through it, we can interact with God in images and symbols, the preferred language of our unconscious Self.

Imagine looking through a large picture window at a scene outside. What kind of scene comes to your mind? A neighborhood, perhaps, or a mountain scene? The beach? A junk yard? Is it attractive or repulsive to you? Do you see it clearly in your imagination, or is it hazy or indistinct? Perhaps you have no visual image at all, but rather a sense of what the scene is. If no scene comes to mind make up a picture of whatever view you would like.

Now imagine going out the door and into the scene, becoming part of the surroundings and participating in the action. Don't worry if it does not seem to happen sponta-

23

neously. Decide what you want to do and just pretend to do it.

Often people tell me that they have no imagination or are not very good with imagery. We all have an imagination and are quite good at using it. The problem is simply that we do not trust our imagination or have limited expectations of what an imaginary experience should be like. We may expect a clear visual picture, which is only one aspect of imagination. Touch, taste, sound, smell and sight, as well as an intuitive sense of presence, mood or action, all belong in the realm of the imagination. We simply need to notice the unique way we each use our imagination—and then trust our Self.

When we look through the picture window of our imagination in prayer, be it a visual or an intuitive picture, we use the favored language of our unconscious Self. We invite and respond to communication with the Spirit at a deep level within our unconscious Self. God speaks to us through our dreams at this same level. We open our self to a wisdom and power as yet unconscious—the movement of the Spirit directing us toward healing and wholeness. Through prayer, we can creatively integrate the deep inner wisdom of our dreams into our conscious life experience.

Let us consider some sources of images and the process of their integration into our spiritual journey. Three phases or movements of imagery in the spiritual life are:

1. forming and choosing the image;
2. playing with the image;
3. integrating the image into the whole picture of our life experience.

The three phases are not clearly delineated; they overlap and we move back and forth among them. They do express a true progression, however, and can be a valuable perspective from which to discern the movements within our prayer and any new inclinations or insights that emerge from our prayer.

Forming and Choosing the Image

The first phase, forming and choosing the image, involves being open to the various images that enter our lives from many sources, allowing them to take shape in our conscious awareness, and choosing one or more on which to concentrate at any given time. It is like placing the image in the frame of a picture window, or watching it form there spontaneously, and then focusing our attention on it. Scripture is one of the richest sources of imagery on which to focus our attention in prayer. The psalms and the books of Isaiah and Jeremiah offer a wealth of images. The four gospels of Matthew, Mark, Luke and John are a special treasure-house for Christian prayer. They contain an abundance of stories to capture our imagination and also provide a setting in which we can interact with Jesus and come to know him more intimately. Building a close personal relationship with Jesus is fundamental to spiritual growth for a Christian, and the gospel stories are the cornerstone of that relationship.

Dreams, as an expression of the Spirit within, are another fundamental source of images for our spiritual life. We all dream, but some of us have difficulty remembering our dreams. Remembering them is obviously the first step in bringing our dreams into our conscious awareness. Here are a few tips to develop our ability to remember our dreams:

1. Before going to sleep, tell yourself you want to remember a dream upon awakening.

2. Place paper and pencil at your bedside to record your dream when you awaken. This can help in strengthening your resolve to remember a dream, as well as being a practical aid and motivation in writing it down. (Even if we remember a dream upon awakening, we tend to forget it if we do not

record at least a few words or phrases to jog our memory later.)

3. Upon awakening, look backward into the night rather than forward into the day. Write down your immediate feelings, thoughts, images or dream fragments. Even if this does not bring more of the dream along with it, the repetition of recording your first impressions is likely to result in remembering a dream within a few days or a week or so.

4. When you do remember a dream, write it out completely as soon as you can. Include details, feelings and actions in the present tense. Then record your immediate reactions to the dream.

When we make an effort to remember and record a dream, we exercise the power of our ego-self to deliberately and consciously choose to be open to our inner Self. In effect, we let our inner Self know we are willing to receive any dream-gift that might be offered to us. We encourage a more intimate relationship between our ego-self and our subconscious Self.

Our lives are filled with images, and God can communicate with us through any and all of them: art in its many forms, music and dance, nature, memories and literature. Images are not limited to visual impressions. They can include sound, touch, taste and smell, as well as impressions of mood and intuition. Feelings lend themselves to imagery, as do relationships. I may feel depressed, as though I am at the bottom of a deep pit; joyful, like a morning in spring; angry as an erupting volcano; serene as a mountain lake. My relationship with a friend may seem distant, as if there were a brick wall or a thick fog between us; or we may feel connected, as if there were a golden thread encircling us. These are only a few examples of the more common and obvious possibilities of imagery within our experience.

The sources of images that can reveal the presence and movement of God in our lives are virtually unlimited.

Playing With the Image

As we consider the various images in our life, we begin to move into the second phase of imagery in our spiritual journey: playing with the image. This phase is at the heart of prayer. When we look through the picture window of our imagination in prayer or go out the door and into the scene, we reach out with open hands to receive a gift from God. When we become absorbed with an image at prayer, we are like a child absorbed in play with a high-quality toy. He or she discovers and develops skills and attitudes in the playing. The child does not need to understand the design of the toy or which particular skills it is meant to develop. The child simply needs to play with the toy and development occurs in the process of the play.

God is like a toy maker who designs a toy for his own child. He knows us, his children, better than we know ourselves. He knows the direction in which we are ready to grow at a given time. He knows what kind of toy will be likely to catch our attention and stimulate our growth as we become absorbed in play. Then he designs an image-toy that will encourage and facilitate our growth and offers it to us as a gift. When we receive his gift and play with it in prayer, God delights in being with us as a loving Father, watching us play and grow.

During our prayer/play time, we need to set aside for the time our urge to understand the meaning of our images and simply immerse ourselves in the process of playing. This may be difficult. We need to let go of the inclination to decide what we should be like and in which direction we should grow. We need to allow God to lead us through our inner Self. We need to be childlike.

How do we play with our images in prayer? We use our imagination and relate to the images like a child with curiosity, a sense of adventure, a willingness to trust and depend on God and allow the Spirit to lead us.

One of the most fruitful ways to play with images is to interact with them actively and consciously in our imagination. We play a role in a dream or a scripture story as if we were an actor in a play. We simply enter the story wherever we choose and interact with the other figures. We allow the story to unfold spontaneously if it will. Or we begin a dialogue or action and see what develops.

Some examples from my own experience may illustrate the use of active imagination in prayer. For instance, on one occasion I chose the story of the healing of the blind beggar (Lk 19:35-43) for prayer. I played the role of the beggar. After taking some time to let the scene take shape in my imagination, and to get in touch with feeling blind and needy, I let the story unfold.

In my prayer, the drama moves along as described in the gospel, up to a point. After the crowd brings me to Jesus, I stand before him and hear him say, "What do you want me to do for you?" At this point the story comes to a dead stop. I find myself paralyzed with fear. I do not have the courage to ask for my sight. I am afraid of what I might see, and afraid of what might happen if I am cured and follow Jesus up the road to Jerusalem. I know that this is Jesus' last journey to Jerusalem, and that he is walking to his passion and death. I stand there in fear for a few very long moments, aware of Jesus' presence and love.

Finally, painfully aware of my cowardice, I ask him for the courage to want to see. Then I am able to ask for and to receive my sight. What I see then is Jesus reaching toward me, inviting me to walk with him to Jerusalem. After a moment of hesitation to summon up my newfound courage, I take his hand and begin to walk with him. He is very grateful and begins to tell me how lonely he is feeling, and how much he needs me to be with him. I put my arm around his waist and he leans on me, seeming tired and burdened. He thanks me for walking beside him and tells me that he feels strengthened and encouraged. I feel overwhelmed, and a sense of disbelief comes over me. How can Jesus need and want *me* to be with him in his time of trial? What do I have to give to him? And yet his message is clear. He needs me and wants me with him. He draws strength from me. And most incredible of all, he loves and trusts me enough to reveal his own human vulnerability to me. I grew dramatically closer to Jesus in this experience.

We can re-enter dreams in our imagination in a similar way. In playing with our dreams in prayer, we open ourselves to receive more deeply and respond more fully to the gift of God contained in the dream. Nightmares, other unresolved or unsatisfactory dreams and recurring dreams tend to be especially fruitful to explore in prayer. They carry special gifts of healing power or courage. It may be difficult to choose a frightening nightmare and be willing to return to it, but it is likely to be a gold mine among dreams. Perhaps an example from my own experience will help to clarify the process as well as to serve as an encouragement to explore your own nightmares.

In my dream, I am being chased at night by a tall, dark man in dark clothes. He has an ax in his hand. He catches me and cuts off both my hands. I look with horror at the bloody stumps of my arms and at my hands lying on the ground in front of me. I am terrified of what he will do next. End of the dream!

I decide to re-enter the dream at the end. But I need some help and protection. I bring Jesus with me to heal my hands back onto my arms. I also bring "Josef," a powerful soldier from a previous dream, to disarm my attacker and restrain him so I can talk to him without fear of further mutilation or death. I want to know what this man wants or needs from me at this particular point in my life. I re-enter the nightmare and it progresses according to my plan at first. Josef takes away the man's ax, holds him down and ties him up. Jesus heals my hands back onto my arms. Mary, the mother of Jesus, is there also.

Then, as I stand facing my attacker, I realize how much I hate him. He looks like a Frankenstein monster. I talk to Jesus and Mary about what a hateful creature he is and how I do not want to talk to him after all. After a long moment, I realize he is a part of me, and I decide to talk to him in spite of my feeling of revulsion.

We form a small circle. I tell my attacker how ugly and horrid he is, and how horrible it was for him to cut off my hands. Arrogantly, he says he is part of me. That makes me furious. I ask why he cut off my hands. He says he likes me when I'm helpless; I do not often look like that. I begin to soften a little. He says I usually look very confident, and he likes to see my insecurity as well. There is now some affection in his voice. I ask his name. He says "Igor," which is a familiar and significant name to me. I suddenly feel very close to Igor. I reach out to take his hand. I sense he wants something else, and I look closely at his face. I ask Igor, "Do you want to help me when I am helpless?" He begins to cry. My question has been answered; that is what Igor wants very much. My monstrous attacker has become a powerful helper. It seems I need only to call on Igor when I feel helpless and he will come to my aid. I have discovered again the special gifts of courage and healing power contained in a nightmare.

We can use our imagination to play actively not only with dreams and scripture stories, but also with other images. We are limited only by our own imagination. Suppose, for instance, I am feeling distant from my spouse or a friend, as if there were a ten-foot-high brick wall between us. I can imagine the wall, touching it and getting a sense of its roughness and its strength. I can ask Jesus or Mary or another spiritual figure to be with me. I can tell him or her how I feel and what I want. I can ask for help to break down the wall or climb over it. Or I may discover something totally unexpected as I talk about my feelings and desires or as I explore the wall.

An excellent source of exercises through which to explore images is the book *Dreams and Spiritual Growth* by Savary, Berne and Williams (Paulist Press, 1984). Most of the exercises can be used effectively with both night dreams and "waking dreams," those imaginary stories generated from other sources, including scripture, memories, feelings, nature, art, literature and music.

One helpful exercise involves writing out an imaginary story or dialogue. For example, we may rewrite all or part of a dream or "waking dream." Writing out a dialogue can surprise us. It may at first seem very contrived, but it typically becomes more free-flowing after the first couple of interchanges. Often we begin to say or ask something surprising and to receive some surprising responses. The surprise element indicates that we are connecting with the Spirit at the level of our unconscious Self.

As we use our imagination in prayer, we may notice images from different sources connecting and interacting. We can learn to follow the direction in which they lead, letting the Spirit guide us from within. An example from my own experience will illustrate this. This experience occurred about a year before the "Igor" ax-man dream, and accounts for the significance of the name to me. This particular series of images originated in a nightmare in which I was afraid of an oriental man who seemed to have great power over me. I summoned up my courage and re-entered the dream to talk with the man. In the conversation we became friends and I found he wanted to help me. I asked his name. He said it was Igor. Surprised, I said that it seemed like an unusual name for an oriental person. He shrugged his shoulders and said he did not like to be predictable! I was quite amused by that; the name certainly caught and held my attention.

Notice the examples of centering and contemplation in

this experience. I became easily Self centered in re-entering the nightmare, due to its emotional power. I stayed with it and allowed myself to be aware of my fear as well as my determination to dialogue with this dream figure. The surprising name indicates the contemplative, deeper nature of the experience; I certainly would never have consciously thought of that name for an oriental man. The name surfaced from my unconscious Self.

The next day, I stopped at the post office to buy some two-cent stamps. I certainly was surprised to see Igor Stravinsky portrayed on the stamps. That image definitely captured my attention, another example of centering. I went on about my shopping, carrying both the actual stamps and the remarkable mental image they presented. I was beginning to feel a sense of adventure.

The next day, I happened to meet with a friend who is very knowledgeable about music. I asked her if she knew what Igor Stravinsky had composed. She could think of only one piece, "Rite of Spring," and suggested that my neighborhood library might have the recording. Though it seemed unlikely, I decided to try anyway, and was surprised to find it there. On my way home with the record, a seemingly disconnected image of a volcano popped into my head. I sensed some link to the music but it was not clear to me at the moment.

I began my prayer the next day with a feeling of foreboding. I intended to listen to "Rite of Spring," and sensed myself on the verge of a powerful experience. I felt the fear of walking into the unknown. It took some courage to start the music. The music did trigger a vivid fantasy, which included participating in a ritual dance in a jungle clearing, being sacrificed by the natives into the mouth of an active volcano, dancing on the surface of the molten lava inside the volcano and finally being shot out of the volcano as it erupted—safely landing in the arms of God as Mother and

Father. The image contains a Self centering, healing power for me as it returns in my memory from time to time.

This shows how music can be used for centering. "Rite of Spring" captured and held my attention easily, and led to a contemplative experience. The deeply contemplative nature of the experience is indicated by the free-flowing and surprising development of the story, with almost no conscious direction on my part, as well as by the enduring and life-giving qualities of the imagery.

The images that surface from our Self do not always seem like images of God at first. In fact, more often than not they seem quite the opposite. Only when we stay and play contemplatively with the image does the dark or hazy film begin to clear away and the face of God become clear. For instance, I certainly did not think of the dream assailant who cut off my hands with an ax as an image of God! The dream at first was more an image of my own horror at finding my self helpless. Both the horror and the helplessness are feelings I do not like to admit. I probably would not have admitted them even then if the vivid nightmare had not captured my attention. My true feelings surfaced as I confronted my assailant. In the same way, the true image of Igor became apparent. While I find my helpless self horrible, Igor finds me lovable. He wants to be with me and help me when I cannot help myself, clearly a true image of God.

A second example of a startling image of God was the oppressive and threatening oriental dream man, the original Igor. Yet when I confronted him, it became apparent that he too really wanted to help me. He triggered a mysterious series of experiences that led to the powerful experience of being caught up into the arms of a strong, nurturing, caring Mother and a powerful, protective, loving Father, another obvious, clear image of God.

A third "face" of God emerged in the only dream I remember from the early years of my life. In the dream, I am looking through the kitchen window into the back yard of my childhood home. It is a sunny day, and the elm tree is spreading a blanket of shade on the lawn. Beyond the tree, in the middle of the lawn, stands a big orange kangaroo.

The dream has come to mind from time to time during the years since my childhood. Each time, I have been intrigued and amused by this picture of an orange kangaroo in my back yard. When I found myself especially attracted to it recently, around the time I first conceived the idea for this book, I decided to return to the scene in my imagination and become acquainted with this wonderful creature. I imagined myself as a little girl, sitting in the shade of the elm tree as I had done so often in my childhood, daydreaming and listening to the cooing of the doves. I watched the kangaroo with delight as she hopped around the yard. Then I walked close to her. She introduced herself as Maggie. She let me look into her pouch where, to my delight, I discovered twin baby kangaroos! Then she gave all three of us a wonderful, bouncing ride around the yard in her pouch.

I have returned to the scene in my imagination occasionally to spend time with Maggie. She is delightful, gentle, playful, strong, protective, understanding and nurturing. She loves me unconditionally, just like God. She brings forth abundant life, just like God. I enjoy her company and she enjoys mine, just like God. I can tell her my innermost thoughts and feelings, and she understands and accepts and loves me, just like God. I had looked through the window of my childhood dream and discovered another image of God.

Maggie expressed aspects of God that were new to me. I had not previously seen God as so joyous and playful, nor thought of God as one who enjoys my company. Maggie had been there since my childhood, but it was not until some 40 years later, when I allowed my attention to be centered on this image of my Self and then stayed to play contemplatively with her, that this new image of God was revealed more fully to me. I drew a picture of Maggie and myself, which hangs on my wall, continuing to bring home to me the joy and delight and love of God.

An orange kangaroo is a unique and unusual image of God. Each of us has within our Self the potential for experiencing our infinite God in a multitude of ways, in a seemingly unlimited variety of shapes and colors and movements. We only need to welcome the images that surface from our inner Self, center our attention on them, stay with them in the drama of contemplative play and watch for the image of God to emerge.

Integrating the Image

When we have played with an image in prayer, when our attention has been centered and we have been absorbed in the drama at a contemplative level, we often sense a natural movement into the next phase. We have a sense of completion, of being finished for now. We don't feel any inclination to play any further; we lose interest as a child does with a toy. The image no longer captures our attention easily; it no longer centers us. We are ready to step away from the image and look at it from a different perspective. It is time to move into the third phase of imagery in the spiritual life: integrating the image into the whole picture of our life experience.

In the third phase, we move out of our subjective immersion in the imagery and step back to view the experience objectively, in the context of our total life experience. It is important to realize that *this is not a time to begin thinking and analyzing.* Imagery does not translate well into analytical thinking; it belongs to a different realm. Playing with images helps us to tap into their power for healing and wholeness. Integration contains and channels the energy released in play. We need to step back and look, as a child steps back and looks at a building just created out of blocks. We need to view it from all sides, noticing anything new that we did not see when we were so close to it. We need to carry it around in our memory and perhaps share it with others, letting it trigger other images or associations or insights.

An example from my own experience may help to clarify the difference between analytical thinking and the kind of integration I encourage at this stage. Let us look at my nightmare of the ax-man attacker and my subsequent return to the scene to ask his name, to make friends and to accept Igor as a helper. I could have begun to analyze the experience by looking at what attribute of mine I might need to change. I might have decided that I was unbalanced toward being too independent, and that I needed to learn to ask for other people's help more often. Then I might have worked on that, trying to change my behavior to be more the way I thought I should be. This would take a lot of energy, it would feel like work and the whole process would probably move very slowly. I would also be likely to experience feelings of frustration and failure along the way. This is what happens when we try to translate imagery into the realm of analytical thinking.

How can I integrate the image within the realm of the imagination? I could simply continue to relate to Igor in the context of my life experience. For instance, suppose I am perplexed with a problem and do not seem to be able to come to any resolution by myself. I happen to be talking to a friend and discuss it with her or him. I see a whole new perspective that helps to resolve the problem. I realize I have changed. I willingly and easily asked for another person's help. I remember Igor and say to him, "Thanks! You helped me to do that, didn't you?!" Igor may just be likely to answer, "You're welcome!"

Or I may remember Igor as I am in the midst of struggling with my problem. I may ask Igor for help, since he said he wants to help me when I feel helpless. He may give me a new perspective that I had not thought of. Or he may suggest that I ask a certain person for help. The point is that *a change has already occurred* within the imaginary play with Igor. Continuing to relate to Igor in the context of my life helps to affirm and to continue the flow of the creative energy from the dream. This enables the Spirit to re-create me from within, according to the movement of my inner Self as opposed to the much more limited perspective of my conscious self.

An excellent initial step from our subjective play toward the more objective integration phase is simply to write a description of our experience, noting our emotions both during the experience and during the writing, as well as any insights or associations that occur. Describe the experience as you would a dream, in the present tense and in as much detail as possible. Writing makes the experience concrete, moving it from our inner to our outer world in a physical, tangible form. We can further express the experience in drawing, painting, poetry, music, dance, sculpture, or any other creative way. In these ways, we can continue to relate to the imagery, with our feet on the ground of concrete, outer reality. We channel the inner creative and healing energy of our Self into our outer, conscious experience, thus integrating it into the whole picture of our life. We thereby encourage the growth of the relationship between our conscious self and our unconscious Self, allowing God to have an ever freer and fuller participation in our continuing creation.

Another excellent way to integrate our inner experience is simply to carry it in our memory as we go about our daily activities, as I integrated my Igor image. The image may come into our consciousness spontaneously and bring an insight or association as it is placed alongside one scene after another of our daily life. It may trigger a new image for us to play with, pointing the way to the next step in our journey.

If we begin to feel as if we are working at integrating

our inner experiences, perhaps getting a headache from thinking and analyzing, or trying to change our behavior to fit the new image, we are probably restricting the flow of the creative energy of the imagery. If a child steps back from a newly created block building and sees a new possibility, he or she might decide to try to make some blocks of different shapes to build the new image. But the child does not possess the ability or the tools, works very hard and ineffectively, and then feels frustrated and discouraged. It would be easier and more effective to ask the toy maker for the necessary new blocks!

Very often in this third phase we gain an insight into what we really are like, and the possibility of what we can become, and then we begin to work at changing ourselves. When we do that, we leave the realm of the imagination and become disconnected from the source of our creative energy. Our ego-self becomes too controlling and limiting. We need to ask God for a new toy that will shape us into what we can become *as we play with it*. When we work at changing ourselves, in a sense we are playing God. We take on the job of our own creation, and that is hard work indeed—God's work. Our part in our creation is to play, and God will re-create us as we play. Our role is to open our hands to the Spirit within, to receive from our Self the image-toy God has made especially for us at this moment of our life, and to play with it. And then to step back and look at the fruit of our play in the context of our life, open our hands again and wait for the next new toy.

THREE

Rattling Windows
Distractions and Feelings

Dealing with distractions and feelings that arise during prayer is a common concern. One kind of distraction can usually be dealt with quite simply. This concerns the busy thoughts that go around in our heads, such as details we need to attend to or plans for coming activities. Sometimes they persist because we are afraid we will forget them: perhaps we need to mail an important letter that day, or maybe a good idea pops into our head that we want to remember. We can tend to these kinds of distractions by simply having paper and pencil handy when we pray and jotting down what we want to remember. We get it off our minds and onto the paper. Then we can center our attention on something more conducive to a contemplative experience.

Another kind of distraction persists despite all our efforts to set it aside. It commonly involves a disturbance in a relationship, either with another person, with God or with a part of ourselves. A typical prayer experience involving this kind of distraction might begin with our choice of a scripture passage on which to focus our attention during a particular prayer period. We may begin to enter into it in our imagination or simply to read it slowly, waiting to see what might catch our attention. But we find we just cannot get into it. We find ourselves involved in a mental conversation with someone, trying to work out a disturbance with the person, rehearsing what we might say. We go around and around in circles with the mental conversation, getting nothing resolved. We may catch ourselves and try to return to the scripture passage, only to find ourselves involved in the mental conversation again. When this kind of distraction persists through our prayer time, we might end our prayer period with a feeling of dissatisfaction, failure and fatigue.

It is as if we were sitting at the window of scriptural prayer and looking with determination for the movement of the Spirit. We work hard and discipline ourselves to stay at that window, trying to ignore the distracting noise of the wind rattling a different window. While we sit there, we may fail to realize that it just might be the Spirit rattling a different window at another side of the house, trying to get our attention and calling us to look at the disturbance in the relationship.

Once we realize that God may be calling us to look more deeply at a relationship, how can we center our attention there? How can we allow the experience to deepen and become contemplative? Let us look at the example above, in which we are involved in an unresolved mental conversation. We begin to center our attention when we simply move to the window that is rattling with the seeming distraction. We let go of our ego-self's initial choice of how to pray and choose instead to follow the movement of the Spirit, which seems to be in a different direction.

Once we have shifted our attention in the new direction, we can look more deeply. Quite often if we notice what we are feeling in the context of our mental conversation, we will find our attention easily focused. Our emotional energy commonly rattles the window and disturbs our quiet. Our surfacing feelings express the dynamic movements of the Spirit within our Self, calling our attention to movements of life and growth. If we simply stop, allow the feeling to surface from within our Self and experience it fully, we enter into it more deeply. For example, we may realize we are angry. If we look beneath the anger, we will usually find fear or hurt or both, along with the anger. As we acknowledge and allow ourselves to feel angry, it can be helpful to ask ourselves what we are afraid of and what has hurt us. As we let ourselves feel the anger and fear and pain in their full intensity, we enter the experience more deeply and become more contemplative.

Along with anger, sexual feelings present most of us with a special challenge. These powerful feelings move us toward outward expression. We may resist feeling them as fully as we might due to family, religious or societal influences that tell us they're unacceptable. Sexual feelings and fantasies, especially, carry strong taboos from our religious institutions, taboos that have arisen from a fear of sexuality. That fear is contagious and many of us have caught it. Fear paralyzes us, and fear of our own sexuality paralyzes our life-giving and creative sexual powers. We can counter our resistance in part by repeatedly reminding ourselves that *feelings* are neither good nor bad. Rather our *response* to our feelings is good or bad, creative or destructive.

Prayer time is prime time to deal with our resistance to anger and sexual feelings. We seem to sense the power of both, and we may be afraid that if we allow ourselves to experience their full strength we will lose control. In fact, the opposite is true. The more we fear and flee our feelings, the more power they have over us. If we repress them, they will surface from our subconscious when we least expect or want them to; we have less control. Feelings ebb and flow

naturally if we do not block them. When we overcome our
fear of their power and courageously acknowledge and experience our feelings, they tend to flow on and diminish.
Then we have more conscious control over our decisions
and actions. We can let our emotional energy flow in and
through our other faculties and enable us to make clearer,
more creative decisions.

Feelings control us in the same way little children do.
When children crave attention, they pester us and get into
mischief to try to get our attention. We cannot get anything
done and the household is anything but peaceful. If we stop
what we're doing and tend to them, listen to them, satisfy
their needs and help find some more appropriate and creative ways to channel their energy, they usually become
contented. Peace and harmony can return.

Powerful feelings distract us by clamoring for attention
and pestering us with a need for expression. Through our
imagination, we can effectively satisfy this tendency of anger
and sexual feelings toward outward expression. We can
imagine doing exactly what we feel like doing without the
restrictions or consequences that would accompany our outer
actions. In the process, we know our emotional self more
clearly, and we channel our wonderfully creative emotional
energy. Peace and harmony can return.

We may be afraid that if we give our feelings free rein
in our imagination, we may discover an unacceptable darkness within ourselves. We all have our dark side, and if we
are to know ourselves as we truly are, we need to summon
up our courage to encounter, accept and embrace our dark
as well as our bright side. We cannot be truly free when we
deny a part of ourselves. It is better to discover our capacity
for violent and destructive thoughts than to perform violent
and destructive acts.

It is better to stab our antagonists in our imagination
than to stab them with a cutting remark when we encounter
them. By addressing the dark side of our feelings through

imagination and fantasy, we recognize and accept that side of ourselves and deal with it in a non-destructive and healing way. Repressed anger has a way of surfacing by causing us to do or say something spontaneously that we would not normally choose; it has power over us. We may say to ourselves: "I can't believe I said that. I wonder what got into me?" What got into us is our mischievous feeling of anger still clamoring for our attention! If we clear the air in our imagination, the energy can be channeled more creatively, perhaps into a very direct conversation with the other person, addressing the problems in our relationship.

In the same way, it is better to discover our capacity for misdirected passion in a sexual fantasy than to engage in sexual actions in an irresponsible and inappropriate way. It is better to fantasize a wild and passionate "forbidden" sexual encounter than to be carried away by passion into a sexual affair that is irresponsible and not freely chosen. Like anger, repressed sexual feelings have a way of surfacing and controlling us. If we clear the air in imaginary sexual fantasy, our wonderful, creative sexual energy can be channeled more constructively, perhaps by openly acknowledging a sexual attraction to another person and freely choosing not to act on it. Then we are in connection with our own creative sexual energy, rather than allowing our sexual passion to control us.

When we repress our anger and sexual feelings, they do not die but rather are buried alive in our subconscious. Besides gaining power over us and diminishing our ability to speak and act freely and responsibly, our repressed feelings can cause internal destruction and wounding. If we do not acknowledge that we are angry enough to stab someone, we may unconsciously stab ourselves, giving rise to inappropriate guilt, depression, lowered self-confidence and decreased energy. We kill some of our own inner life. If we do not acknowledge the strength of our sexual energy and passion, if we inhibit the flow of our sexual feelings and fantasies, we restrict the life-giving power of our sexuality, directed toward union and new birth, both inward and outward. I encourage you to trust your Self to experiment. Welcome free-flowing sexual fantasy as part of your prayer and then notice the result. You may be surprised to find you feel more in touch with who you are as a woman or as a man. You may feel a new ease and creativity in your interactions with members of the opposite sex. You may feel an increase in your creative energy. All of these commonly result when we drop our inner sexual inhibitions and connect with the abundant creative life embodied in our sexual natures.

Feelings surface from deep within our Self and express the movements of the Spirit. They present our true and authentic Self, not who we think we are or should be in a given situation. When we allow any and all of our emotions to surface uncensored and then experience them fully until they are spent, we engage ourselves with the life and movement of the Spirit within. We are likely to come to a calmer place. From here we can see the truth of the situation more clearly and act with greater freedom and authenticity. We are able to stop spinning our wheels by trying to analyze the situation or by chattering to our self in endless mental conversation, going around in circles and getting nowhere, working hard and exhausting ourselves in the process. When we let go and sink deeply into the feelings moving in the situation, we let God do the work, and we open our self to the wisdom and truth of the Spirit revealed within the experience.

Another way to look more deeply at a relationship that has attracted your attention is to see if any specific moment of interaction with the person seems to be lingering. If so, draw a cartoon of the other person's face, depicting your impression of the feelings and attitude of the person. If you remember a statement or two that he or she made at the moment, write it next to the image. It is not necessary to quote the person exactly. Your memory or impression of the meaning of the statements will be more helpful. Then draw a frame around the picture. Imagine that it is a mirror, and you are looking at a reflection or projection of your Self. Look closely at the image. Look at the picture as it is, not as you intended it to look. Usually, a cartoon picture looks different from the image we have in our mind. It is a new image, probably influenced by the inner artist in our subconscious Self. Notice if the image triggers an association with any other experience in your life, perhaps with a different relationship. If it does, shift your attention to that relationship and allow it to become contemplative.

An example from my own experience may help to clarify this process of uncovering an elusive projected image, as well as to illustrate its value and effectiveness. A young woman had shared with me her difficulty in seeing the suffering of several members of her family, but being helpless to do anything to alleviate their pain. She felt a deep sadness, and tears overflowed as she spoke of the situation. I was puzzled by the way her face lingered in my memory and I was unable to shake it. For several days I noticed it, but did not think it was significant. Finally, I decided it might be asking for attention from me.

I drew a cartoon picture of her sad face with tears streaming down her cheeks. After drawing a frame around it, I wrote three lines alongside it: "I can't fix it"; "sad"; "helpless." I looked at it as if it were a mirror.

As I looked at it, I realized that it reminded me of my own feelings toward a close friend who was in pain and unable to find healing. I had tried to help her, but could not "fix it" for her. She had come to mind recently, bringing tears of sadness to me. I felt frustrated and had many mental conversations with her, trying to help. These conversations were a waste of time and energy and they were helping no one. When I owned my true helplessness, I was able to let go of trying to control the situation and to acknowledge that it was simply sad. I was free to direct my energy in more effective directions. I also found that I felt more supportive and accepting toward my friend.

Another window that commonly rattles during prayer is our attic window; like the other rattling windows, it usually seems like an undesirable distraction. The attic is the place of memories. Sometimes we need to tend to an unresolved experience from our past, perhaps an event we would prefer to forget. Yet it persists in our memory, sometimes coming to consciousness in prayer. Its persistent recurrence indicates that the Spirit may be rattling our attic window to get our attention and invite us to look at the experience at a new level, deeper within our Self.

Such an experience arose for one woman during her retreat. She was having difficulty in her relationship with her father, and hoped for a peaceful, refreshing retreat in which she could set aside the disturbances in the relationship. She felt restless and agitated when she tried to focus her attention in prayer, however. She could not get her father off her mind. When we met, she told me of a painful memory of a past incident with her father. The memory persisted in spite of her efforts to set it aside. It was obviously excruciatingly painful for her to remember. I suggested that the Spirit might be inviting her to look more deeply at this incident, rather than to pray in the peaceful way she would prefer. I encouraged her to return to the scene in her imagination and to say or do what she was not able to at the time the incident occurred, perhaps writing out a dialogue.

She was quite reluctant, but agreed to try. When we met the next day, she told me she had returned to the scene and found much deeper feelings of hurt and anger than she had expected. It was an intensely painful experience, and I had great admiration for her courage. She felt guilty for having such strong feelings about her father. She was able to overcome this inappropriate guilt and accept her true feelings as they emerged from her Self. She experienced her Self as she truly was, rather than as she thought she should be. She discovered that she felt a deep compassion for herself that was new for her. She found a power for healing within her Self that enabled her to care for herself and to be more loving in her relationship with her father. When she was able to love her Self as she truly was, she was also able to see and love her father as he truly was. Only when she courageously chose to trust her Self, to look through the rattling attic window of her memory, was she able to be healed at a deeper level. She was able to let the Spirit lead her to the peaceful and loving place that she desired.

Another window that sometimes rattles distractingly during prayer is our basement window. The basement is a repulsive place of darkness and shadow, spiders and snakes, trash and junk. We do not easily agree to look at the dark side of ourselves. Yet out of the darkness of a mine gold comes forth. Out of the darkness of the tomb new life emerges. It takes courage to acknowledge the rattling of our basement window, but when we open it the light is allowed to shine in and the bright side of our shadow can be revealed. The hidden treasure can be discovered.

Another woman's retreat experience illustrates the value of this kind of distraction. On the last day of her retreat, Cathy told me she remembered a dream from several months previously. The memory was persistent and remained quite vivid. The dream's setting was a dining room. She stood in the doorway, looking in at a rattlesnake coiled on the table. Her dream ended there. She had a strong aversion to snakes, and did not even want to consider dealing any more with this dream. We talked about what she could do to feel safe enough to re-enter the dream and confront the snake. She began to consider some possibilities. I encouraged her to follow through with it, pointing out that the more we fear something the more power it has over us.

Not long after the retreat I received a note from Cathy, in which she shared with me the next episode of the story. She did in fact return to the doorway of the dining room to meet the snake. Jesus stood by her side. As she wondered what to do, suddenly the snake uncoiled and flung himself across the room like a wet dishcloth and landed across her arms. She was shocked and frozen. After a moment, she recovered enough to ask his name, and then what he was bringing her or what he wanted from her. The snake was immediately transformed into a lamb. He said that he had come to bring her the gift of play. I admired her courage and shared her joy in the wondrous gift she had received.

Only when Cathy made a conscious and courageous decision to trust her Self and to open her rattling basement window was her fearful image of the snake transformed into the delightful and playful lamb. During her retreat, she had expressed a desire to be more playful, and the Spirit responded with this lovable little lamb to show her the way. All she needs to do now is to play with him as God watches with delight!

When we are willing to center our attention on our persistent distractions in prayer and allow them to become contemplative experiences, we are likely to discover that what had seemed like a barrier is really a prayer window made of pure gold. What we may have perceived as a worthless distraction may in fact be a rich source of growth to which the Spirit is calling us. We would do well to turn our attention in the direction of our persistent distractions and to explore them in depth. We may discover a surprise gift from God, disguised in a wrapping that gives little hint of the treasure inside. God does seem to delight in surprising us, especially when we least expect it!

Sometimes a feeling will surface in prayer as a vague stirring, seemingly disconnected from any specific event. We may feel depressed, or slightly restless. Prayer may seem generally dry or boring, sometimes for an extended period of time. It is like sitting in the middle of our house at the beginning of a prayer time with no attraction to any prayer window and no idea where to begin. At such times, we can focus on the feeling itself, letting it lead us. As we sit in stillness and let the feeling develop, we might in time be able to give some expression to it. We may realize we feel depressed, discontented, restless, bored, confused, lost, helpless. Perhaps we cannot name the feeling but we can express it in an image. Maybe we feel like a child wandering in the desert or a dense forest, lost and alone. Or perhaps we feel like we are in a dark cave or a dark pit and cannot find our way out. We may realize that we feel distant or disconnected from God. This may lead us to be in touch with sadness and with a deep longing for God. The images can be explored as we wait and watch for God's movement and direction. In fact, we are likely to be led to God through our engagement in the imagery.

At other times, a feeling that is at first vague may develop into an intense emotion, such as anger or fear or hurt. It may lead us directly to an experience in which we did not realize we felt so strongly. We can center on the feeling and allow it to deepen and intensify until it is spent. Then, as with the feelings at the center of a persistent distraction, we may see the direction in which the Spirit is calling us to move.

Feelings are signs of life and movement within. They are valuable expressions through which God can reveal the truth to us about who we really are and how the Spirit is moving within us.

A word about tears. Tears are a precious gift in prayer. They are the overflowing of our feelings. Their presence is a sign of life. They help us to become like soft clay in God's hands, yielding willingly to God's touch. As they overflow and find their course down our cheeks and fall to the ground, they help us to let go of our own attempts to control who we think we should be. They help us to see ourselves as lovable little children—the way God sees us—and to let God's love flow over and around us, surrounding us and carrying us.

Let us welcome our distractions, our feelings and our tears as precious signs of God's presence and movement within our Self. Let us center our attention on them, following our feelings in the direction the Spirit leads from within our own depths. And let us allow our tears to soften us to receive the gentle touch of God's love.

FOUR

Stained Glass Windows
Scriptural Prayer

The scriptures deserve special attention in any consideration of Christian prayer. Like the stained glass windows of a church, they immediately connect us with a rich and deep tradition. They express the spiritual experience of the people of God—people who have allowed their lives to be touched and transformed by the Spirit of God. As such, the scripture stories contain archetypal elements: images and movements common to all of us—typical—that can touch and change, heal and empower us. When we open our own stained glass window of scriptural prayer, we open ourselves to the same transforming Spirit of whom our spiritual ancestors speak so eloquently through their many-colored and variously shaped stories. Their stories are our stories, both as a people and as individuals. The scriptures have a special power to connect with the Spirit within our Self, to come to life in prayer and to lead us to new life and transformation.

51

The four gospels of Matthew, Mark, Luke and John have a unique value beyond the powerful archetypal figures and stories they contain. First of all, they provide a base to develop a personal relationship with Jesus—settings wherein we can interact with Jesus and a starting point from which our relationship with him can grow ever more intimate and dynamic.

The growth of our personal relationship with Jesus has important implications for our spiritual journey. Jesus is a primary guide for us on the journey. It is vital that we be able to trust him. As we come to know him more intimately, we can trust him more deeply, and we can grow more open and more willing to follow him. Our fear diminishes and our courage increases; we accept his guidance and his challenges more readily.

The gospels have another unique value in regard to prayer. They provide a point of reference from which we can step back and view our subjective, personal relationship with Jesus with some objectivity. They paint a portrait of Jesus through the accounts of his actions and words. We can place our own personal, subjective portrait of Jesus alongside the objective gospel portrait and look for the similarities and differences. The comparison can bring to light any distortions that might have been incorporated into our personal image of Jesus—distortions that can obscure the true image of Jesus and unconsciously block the growth of our relationship with him.

A couple of examples may help to clarify this process. I came to prayer on one occasion feeling ashamed of myself and judging myself quite harshly for something I had done. I sat with Jesus, telling him how rotten I was. After I finished chastising myself, I stopped and looked at Jesus. I was startled to see him staring at me in a very cold and judgmental way. He said nothing. I instinctively turned my attention from the experience. This was not the forgiving, loving Jesus I had come to know through the gospels. Something was not right. I was perplexed by the experience. I had never before experienced Jesus this way in any of my interactions with him in prayer. After discussing the experience with my spiritual director, it became clear that I had looked at Jesus through the distorted "glass" of my own judgmental and unforgiving self, so strong at the time that Jesus' true, forgiving Spirit was unable to shine through from my inner Self.

A similar experience arose in a young woman during a spiritual direction meeting with me. She was telling me how she was unable to be the way she wanted to be, unable to let go. She was becoming painfully aware of her limitations as she spoke. It became increasingly evident to me that she felt helpless to change and found it difficult to accept her human limitations. She did not find herself lovable in this situation. I asked her how she thought Jesus might respond to her if he were standing before her at the moment, looking at her just as she was describing herself. She said, with an impatient tone of voice, "He'd probably say, 'Just let go!' " I asked if she thought Jesus would find her lovable at that moment. Her eyes filled with tears. She said she knew in her head that he would find her lovable, but she did not yet know it in her heart. She had discovered the distortion of her own judgmental, unforgiving attitude toward herself, just as I had in the previous example. She took a step closer to Jesus as she caught a glimpse of the distortion alongside what she knew was a truer picture of Jesus—the gospel portrait of Jesus as one who finds us lovable just the way we are and wants to be with us in our helplessness.

Jesus in the gospels is a touchstone whereby we can evaluate not only our personal, subjective experiences of Jesus himself, but any of our spiritual experiences. He is a reference point for us in our attempt to discern whether it is the Spirit of God leading us or a deceptive or evil spirit. Jesus embodies and manifests the Spirit of God in his ac-

tions, his words, his life, his presence. As we get to know
Jesus personally and intimately, we gradually discard our
distorted images of him and allow his true Spirit to emerge.
We come to know his characteristic attitudes and actions. In
the process, we recognize God's characteristic attitudes and
actions more clearly.

The gospel portrait of God as expressed in and through
the person of Jesus is a picture of . . .

> a God who loves us totally and unconditionally,
>> just the way we are at any given moment,
>>> not the way we think we should be . . .
>
> a God who forgives us even before we realize
>> we need to be forgiven . . .
>
> a God who wants us to be healed and whole and happy,
>> who enjoys surprising us with lavish gifts . . .
>
> a God who wants to be with us in suffering and in joy,
>> in victory and in defeat,
>>> in sickness and in health,
>>>> in imprisonment and in freedom,
>>>>> in death and in resurrection.

Any spiritual experience in which an image of God
seems to be the opposite of this gospel portrait is more likely
coming from the limited, distorted perspective of our ego-
self than from the clear, true depths of our inner Self. If we
follow the gospel way of Jesus, we follow the way of the
cross—passion, death and resurrection. We must let our
ego-self's limited and distorted images of God die, painful
as that might be, and allow the true Spirit to rise from the
depths of our unconscious Self, bringing us to new life. This
frequently means that we need to take a longer, deeper
contemplative look at an image that seems obviously distorted. The distorted image must die for the true image of
God to rise. This often calls for courage in the face of fear;
it can be painful.

My "Igor" experiences are examples of this process. It

was painful and frightening for me to confront images that seemed to be sources of pain and oppression—certainly the opposite of the gospel portrait of an all-loving God. I needed to look deeper than this first impression. Confronted in contemplative prayer, the images were transformed. The initial images died and the true images of the God who finds me lovable and who wants to be with me in my confusion and helplessness could emerge from the depths of my Self. The transformed images of Igor look remarkably like the gospel portrait of God revealed in and through Jesus. We need to stay with our experiences, allowing them to deepen, to become centered and contemplative. Out of this dark "tomb" the Spirit of God can arise, dispel the darkness and distortion, and move with us and in us to freedom and new life.

When we choose a scriptural passage on which to center our attention in prayer, it helps to approach it in ways that tend to move us into Self centered, contemplative prayer. We need to *allow our self to be moved from within by the scriptural word of God.* In that way, we will be less likely to pray in an ego-self centered way, consciously trying to *move the word into the place we think it should fit in our life.*

The following basic framework might be used in praying with scripture. Experiment with it; seek ways that bring you to Self centered prayer. Trust your Self as you search for and explore your own unique ways.

1. Before your prayer time, perhaps on the previous day, choose a scripture passage and read it over once or twice or simply let a familiar passage or story rise up from your memory or focus on a story that has come to mind recently and is attracting your attention.

2. Begin your prayer time by taking time to become comfortable, attentive and relaxed, in whatever way is effective for you. For example, you might focus your attention on your breathing, your body sensations, the sounds around

you, a candle, or a mantra. If you find yourself unable to relax or focus your attention within a short time, simply move on. Sometimes the way you choose to pray with the scripture passage will provide a more effective way to center your attention.

3. Read the passage again, slowly, or simply recall the story as you remember it. Notice any part that attracts your attention or causes any emotions to surface.

4. Choose a way to encourage the passage to affect you more deeply. Suggestions:

a. If a sentence / word / phrase attracts you, repeat it over and over, perhaps shortening it as you do, until only a single short phrase or one word remains. Repeat it in rhythm with your breathing.

b. Read the passage as a letter addressed to you, inserting your name, for example, in place of "Israel" or "my people." If appropriate, read it as though it is really being said by you, using your words and feeling your emotions. Many of the psalms lend themselves to this approach.

c. Participate in the scene in your imagination. You may choose to take the role of one of the figures in the scene or to stand beside one of them, or to be an animal or inanimate object. Participate as fully and actively as possible and let the scene unfold freely in your imagination. Continue beyond the end of the passage if desired. Use all of your senses: sight, sound, smell, touch, taste. Write it out if that is helpful. The gospel stories lend themselves well to this imaginative way of prayer.

d. Notice whether any associations occur to you—a connection with an event in your life or a feeling or attitude. Shift your attention to the event or feeling, or incorporate it into the scripture passage if appropriate. Allow yourself to experience it more deeply and fully.

Pay special attention to any feelings that surface during any of these prayer experiences. Allow the feelings to surface fully and to grow. Pause to experience them deeply, and perhaps allow them to lead you in a new direction.

5. Express your feelings and reactions to the Lord. Be attentive. Listen to the Lord. Respond. Write out the dialogue if that is helpful.

6. Be still in God's presence. Be open and receptive.

Feel free to move back and forth among steps 3, 4, 5 and 6.

7. Take a few minutes after your prayer time to write down your experience in a journal. Make special note of any feelings that arose during your prayer, and how you feel about your experience now. You may wish to express your experience in an art form—such as clay, crayon, paint, felt pens— as part of your next prayer time.

Let the scriptures be a starting point, allowing yourself to be moved by the word beyond the limits of the actual passage. For instance, a psalm may be very moving and may inspire you to go beyond the text and to continue in your own words, writing your own psalm. An example of this is "My Psalm," included at the end of the book as an Epilogue.

Another example occurred for me when I chose the Christmas story as a starting point for one prayer time during Advent. I entered the scene of Jesus' birth in my imagination. I became very interested in the manger itself. I touched it, noticing especially the roughness of the wood. I looked around at those gathered in the stable. I found myself attracted to the black king, Balthazar. I went over to him and knelt beside him. I was surprised to find a little lamb lying next to him. He was resting his hand gently on the lamb. I was struck simultaneously by the strength of his hand and the tenderness of his touch.

I spent much of my prayer time during that Advent season getting to know Balthazar. The more intimately I came to know him, the more qualities of the gospel portrait of Jesus I found. He was totally loving, compassionate, powerful, tender, challenging. The more I trusted him, the more truly he led me to fuller life and love.

Several months later, I chose the story of the Good Samaritan to begin my prayer time. I took the role of the wounded traveler and lay beside the road, wounded and helpless. The Good Samaritan came along, and I was surprised to see that he was Balthazar. This wondrous image of God was certainly not limited to the original scripture story of the Nativity! He had returned with his gentle, powerful, healing touch to bring me to new life again. He challenged me to acknowledge a wound that was deeper than I knew, and then healed me with his tears of compassion and his tender touch.

Recently Balthazar returned to take a dominant role in my prayer experience once again. He remained a central figure for several weeks, leading me as usual in the direction of the Spirit. At one time during this period, I began to think something was wrong. Balthazar was a stronger figure for me than Jesus, and I began to think Jesus should be more dominant in my prayer. I decided to talk it over with Jesus, and to tell him of my concern. His response was immediate and to the point. He said, "Silly! Where do you think Balthazar came from? Don't you know he is a gift from me? Just stop worrying and enjoy his company. Trust him. He will lead you along the right path." Jesus' reply strengthened an already deep conviction of mine: God is not limited to any particular image, not even the image of Jesus. Any spiritual experience consistent with the gospel portrait of God is a gift that leads in the direction of the Spirit of God, which is always the direction of healing and wholeness.

A diversity of spiritual experience—including but not limited to scriptural prayer—enriches and deepens our relationship with God. The scriptural stained-glass-window portrait of God has segments of various shapes and colors. The light of the Spirit shines through the whole window.

Each of our spiritual experiences is like one facet of God. It does not matter which particular segment we are looking through at any given moment. What does matter is whether or not it fits into the overall portrait of God as revealed in and through Jesus in the gospels. If our segment distorts the true image of God, it will not fit harmoniously into the whole picture. We may be able to see the distortion if we step back to look at the entire window. If our segment is clear and undistorted, it will not only fit into the picture with ease, but it will add a rich new depth and color to the portrait—and to the way we see our God.

FIVE

Bay Windows
Outward Expressions

Some ways of prayer are like bay windows, expanding outward, extending beyond the walls of the house. These outer or physical expressions of inner movements of prayer include art forms such as drawing and painting, sculpture and pottery, music and dance and body movements, poetry and other creative writing.

Imagine a bay window with an inviting window seat. Sit in it. Notice how much wider your view is. You are still inside the house, yet in a sense you are outside it, beyond the boundary of the main walls. The expressive, creative inclination or urge of outward directed prayer seems to move in rhythm with the inner movements of our Self, flowing with them in a single stream, moving beyond the inner boundaries to an outward expression—inside and outside at the same time. The outward-moving forms of prayer give a new and wider view of the inner experience. They are

tangible, visible, audible expressions of the life and movement of the Spirit within.

Creative, artistic forms of prayer are not just for the
trained and talented artist but for all of us. We each have
an inner artist and dancer and musician. We each have a
body that longs to be free, to speak of who we are and of
how God is moving in us. In order to release our artistic
inclinations, we must become like a little child who can
dance and move and paint and play freely, without inhibi-
tion, without worrying about the "right" way to do it. We
must set aside our adult expectations, the limited views of
our ego-self. Then in a simple, childlike way we can follow
the urgings of our unlimited inner Self and express them in
a free-flowing outward direction.

Artistic prayer forms can bring more freedom and life
to our communication with God. Praying in new ways helps
to break old patterns, which may have slowly and subtly
become blockages. When we pray in the same way over a
period of time, we may unconsciously develop ways of controlling our prayer. Prayer becomes more ego-self centered
and controlled, less Self centered. It becomes more difficult
to discern the surprises and movements of the Spirit. Not
only does a change help to break the pattern, but the very
nature of art makes it less subject to our control. Art is
concerned with imagery and physical expression, which we
cannot control as easily as our thoughts.

Let us consider some simple, childlike ways in which
we can use art forms as prayer. Drawing is an easy way to
begin. Crayons or felt pens and a sheet of paper are all you
need to get started. Assembling the materials is easy. Most
of us will find it harder to approach the materials as a child
would, playing with them instead of working at producing
something. We may need to practice a bit and use our imagination. Imagine being a little child, and explore what a
crayon or felt pen is like, what it will do on paper, how it
feels. Scribble a picture. Enjoy it. Draw or paint whatever

you want. You may want to express a feeling, or an image. Let the crayon or felt pen have a say in what the picture is like.

There is another very simple way to nurture a childlike attitude in drawing. Choose four crayons, two warm colors and two cool colors if you wish. Or close your eyes and take four crayons from the box. Take one of the crayons, close your eyes, and draw a doodle on the paper. Look at it and notice if it suggests any image. If it does, you may want to use the other colors to embellish and develop the image. If no image emerges, simply complete the picture as an abstract drawing in any way you wish. Try to let the picture tell you when it is finished. Or you might want to close your eyes for the entire picture, using one color after another, letting the crayons and your fingers tell you when the picture is complete.

Then look at your completed picture. Notice how you feel about it. Recall how you felt during the process of drawing it. Put the picture in a place where you will see it occasionally. Notice any feelings that arise when you look at it. Notice any images that emerge from it that you did not see before.

A couple of examples from my own experience will illustrate some of the possibilities of this process of "blind doodling." One such picture began with a few swirls in a rust-brown color and some in light blue. I looked at the doodle for a while, seeing no particular image. Then I noticed a part that looked like the head of a dolphin. As I continued to look, I saw the suggestion of a whole dolphin leaping out of the water. I filled in the dolphin's body, added fins, and extended the blue swirls to make waves. I ended up with a picture of two of my favorites among God's creatures—the dolphin and the ocean—in wonderful, powerful, harmonious motion. I was delighted with this special gift. I felt a renewed childlike openness, freedom and joy.

Another example of blind doodling is a picture I drew

during a retreat weekend. I began with a red crayon and drew a few swirls with my eyes closed. No particular image suggested itself as I pondered my doodle, so I simply embellished the original lines with the other colors, enjoying the creation of an abstract design. I sensed when the picture was finished, and then I set the crayons aside and pondered my creation. I turned the picture around and discovered a heart. The heart did not strike any particular chord in me at the time. I was simply pleased with the picture, and had enjoyed the process.

Alone at home on Monday morning, in the quiet of prayer, feelings began to surface—feelings that I had set aside during the busy time of the weekend, when I needed to focus on my role as a facilitator. They were feelings of hurt, confusion and anger that arose from my interactions with a friend during the retreat. When I looked again at my doodle-picture from the weekend, I was amazed at what I now saw. There was my wounded heart. When I turned the picture around, there was an angry red explosion. The feelings that had not surfaced consciously during the retreat had found their expression unconsciously as I playfully doodled! The picture helped me to acknowledge my feelings, to recognize their intensity and depth, and to summon up the courage to share my experience with my friend.

Creative writing is another outward-moving form of prayer that can be fruitful at times. It is important to distinguish writing with a finished product in mind from writing as a free and spontaneous expression. The more free-flowing the writing is, the more it tends to center our attention and become contemplative. Poetry in the style of the psalms lends itself to prayer. It can be extremely moving to write your own psalm, perhaps incorporating familiar lines from the scriptural psalms. (See "My Psalm" in the Epilogue.)

Making up a story can be an effective prayer activity. Once I decided to make up a scary and gruesome nightmare to use as an illustration during a day of dream exploration with a group. When I explored my "waking nightmare" in active imagination, I discovered a surprising depth of feeling and meaning. When we simply write what we feel like writing, we are likely to tap into the movement of the Spirit at a depth we could not have anticipated. It is such a childlike and deceptively simple way, but many of us tend to think we should have to work harder than that to be in touch with the Spirit of God! However, when we become childlike and playful, our ego-self controls and defenses are down and we are more open to God's actions within our Self.

Creative writing is not necessarily limited to poetry and stories. Writing is a very common and easy way to become centered at prayer. I have a friend who is married, has four children between the ages of 3 and 16 years, and has a full-time job outside her home. She prays in solitude by going into her bedroom for a time and closing the door, after making a "Do not disturb" request of the family. She was having difficulty focusing her attention because of the household noises. She played environmental tapes, such as sounds of the ocean surf, to block out the distracting noise. She found it still took a long time to become centered. Then she tried writing whatever came to mind and whatever feelings surfaced. She responded in whatever direction the writing seemed to lead. She found that she no longer needed to play the tapes. The writing centered her attention so effectively that the noises no longer distracted her. She discovered what it means to "Pray as you can, not as you can't."

This kind of writing can be very creative and contemplative, an effective way to open ourselves to the movement of the Spirit within our Self. When we listen and watch contemplatively as we write, we can let go of our ego-self control in our writing and be open to our deeper Self. One way to encourage this openness is to pause from time to time, look at what you have written, and notice how you feel. Writing focused on thinking tends to be ego-self centered. Feelings tend to emerge from our deeper Self. Stay with the feelings and explore them. For example, you might write something like, "I feel sad and rejected, like a little girl who did not receive an invitation to the birthday party of a neighborhood child." Then write how you imagine yourself as the little girl reacting to this situation. Perhaps you are sitting alone in your room and crying while you hold your favorite teddy bear in your arms.

Dialogue is especially effective in beginning or continuing our connection with our inner Self, particularly as we write the responses. You might, for instance, begin to write a dialogue with the little girl and find a surprising reply from her.

It seems easier for us to write a monologue than a dialogue in prayer. We believe that we can speak to the Lord through our own writing, but do we believe that the Spirit could speak to us through our own writing? Yet in *paying attention to the responses*, we are most likely to come in touch with the direction of the Spirit within our Self. Listen to the replies that emerge from the Lord or another figure with whom you are dialoguing. Watch your surfacing feelings. Look at any images that surface during the writing. We may need to decide to try it and then see if the responses that we write seem to come from our deeper Self and are consistent with the image of God as portrayed by Jesus in the gospels.

Clay sculpture is another simple way of artistic prayer. As with writing and drawing, it is important to approach the clay in a simple, childlike way. Explore the clay as a little child would. Take some time to discover what it is like, and what you can do with it. You might shape it into whatever you feel like making, but it is important to set aside any expectations of what you think it should look like when finished. Let the clay tell you when it has become what it wants to be. As you ponder the finished sculpture, notice how you feel about it.

Another approach is to "absent-mindedly" shape the

clay as you listen to some music, or allow your attention to center on a "distraction" or a feeling, or perhaps carry on a dialogue with the Lord. When you remember the clay in your hands, you might look at what shape it has taken. An image may suggest itself in the clay, and you may want to smooth it out or refine it, letting the clay tell you when to stop. It would not be unusual for the image that emerges to be a further and often surprising expression of the more conscious prayer activity on which your attention was focused. At that point, the sculpture would likely become the center of your attention. Gazing at the clay creation, and perhaps touching and caressing it further, could deepen your contemplative experience.

Body movement and dance can be unique ways to express our true Self, to be with God as we truly are at the moment and experience the movement of the Spirit of God revealed to us through our own body language. As with crayons or paints or clay, a good first step is to become acquainted with the material, in this instance our own body. We can get to know our body by simply sitting still and focusing on the various sensations that we do not normally notice when we are moving. Begin at the top of your head and spend a few seconds on each part of your body, from head to toe, noticing the obvious as well as the subtle sensations—tension and looseness, itching and tingling, aching places and comfortable places. Try not to move. Just notice. Move your attention from head to toe several times, as long as your interest is held. Observe new or more pronounced sensations that you did not notice during the previous cycle.

After a time, look for any part of your body that seems to want to move. Let it move as much as it wants. Experiment. Try to let your body tell you what it wants to do. Get up and move and stretch any way your body seems to feel inclined. Find out what your body likes and what it is able to do.

We can also become better acquainted with our bodies

by dialoguing with them. We can dialogue in imagination
or writing, with our entire body or one part at a time. For
example, we might begin by telling our body how we feel
about it, what we want of it, what we need from it. Then
it is very important to imagine or write the response of our
body. Continue the dialogue until it seems to be finished
for the time.

Sometimes our body may initiate a dialogue by getting
our attention through discomfort such as a stomachache, a
pain in the neck, tension in our shoulders, grinding of our
teeth, a cramp in our leg. It may be trying to tell us there
is something we cannot "stomach"; that something or someone is a "pain in the neck"; that we are trying to "shoulder"
more than we can bear; that we have "bitten off more than
we can chew"; that we are running away from something
we need to face. Our body may also simply be telling us
that we need to rest. By dialoguing with it, we can learn to
discern with increasing clarity the messages it sends us. God
can speak to us through our bodies as well as any other
medium, and we would do well to learn to listen more and
more contemplatively to God's bodily revelations to us.

We can initiate or continue a dialogue with God through
our body in dance movements. One simple way is to listen
to whatever music you want and to move with the music.
Try to let your body have a say about how to move; follow
its promptings. Dancing can be a profoundly contemplative
way of communicating with God without words or images,
but in the simple, expressive movements and sensations of
our bodies in rhythm with the music.

Let us run to God in prayer like a child with open arms . . .
        searching eagerly for the window where God is
        calling . . .
                playing hide-and-seek awhile . . .
        and then discovering a window where a new toy
        awaits . . .
                an image . . . a feeling . . . a movement.

Let us explore . . . center . . . contemplate . . .
> be our Self . . . become our Self.

Let us allow God to show us who we are today . . .
> a playful imp . . . a wounded heart . . .
>> a frightened child . . . a courageous hero . . .
>
> a passionate lover . . . a graceful dancer . . .
>> a rejected friend . . . a helpless infant . . .
>
> a serene companion . . . a nurturing mother . . .
>> a solid rock . . . a furious dragon . . .
>
> a leaping stag . . . a gentle doe . . .
>> a lost sheep . . . a caring shepherd.

As we discover the mystery of the life within our Self . . .
> let us stand reverently and behold the image of
> God . . .
>> God, reflected in our deepest, truest Self . . .
>
> the Spirit of God passionately living, loving,
> moving . . .
>> in our imagination . . . our feelings . . .
>>> our body . . . our Self . . .
>>>> one with us . . . holy . . . whole.

SIX

Self, Ego-self and God
Discernment and Direction

In its multicolored and variously shaped forms, prayer constantly involves the process of discerning the direction in which God is inviting us to turn. Discernment is a matter of perceiving, discovering, noticing and recognizing the movements of the Spirit in our lives. It means being in touch with and being guided by the Spirit of God as we make the many decisions that determine the directions we will take along the journey of our life. Some of the choices we make occur at major forks in the road; some are minor alternate routes; some are detours. All require decisions and involve discernment.

At the heart of the discernment process is the interaction between our conscious self and our unconscious Self. Here, at the juncture between our limited, conscious ego-self and our seemingly unlimited, unconscious inner Self, discernment becomes contemplative. Here the strength of our ego-self is of paramount importance. Here we need to use our ego-self's ability to consciously and courageously make the choice to let go of our limitations and control and to be open to the infinite wisdom, power and creativity of the Spirit of God within our Self.

It is the moment of trust . . .
> The moment of faith in a Power
> > infinitely greater than our own . . .
> The moment of dying to self in the hope of resurrection
> > to new life, new vision, new possibilities . . .
> The moment of surrendering love,
> > the choice to be vulnerable and open to
> > > an intimate encounter with our Divine Lover.

It is the moment of contemplation.

When our discernment is contemplative, when we are in touch with and guided by the Spirit of God, we can make major and minor decisions that will most likely be life-giving for ourselves and for the other people in our lives. We live our lives more fully, more in harmony with our authentic Self. The Spirit of God flows in and through us more creatively and abundantly and freely.

Let us look more closely and specifically at the process of discernment in prayer. We will consider discernment in three areas of prayer similar to the three phases of imagery discussed in Chapter Two. First of all, we practice discernment at the beginning of a prayer period, when we try to discover from which prayer-window the Spirit might be calling or whispering to us. Secondly, we practice discernment during the heart of our prayer when we allow ourselves to participate fully, deeply, contemplatively in our prayer experience, and again when we sense it is time to move outward. A third area of discernment occurs as we integrate our prayer experience into our total life, noticing the ways it falls into place and joins the direction and flow of our outer life.

At the beginning of prayer, as we consider which form of prayer to choose, we can practice discernment by looking beyond our ego-self and toward our inner Self for a clue such as a feeling or image or inclination that attracts our attention to a particular way of prayer. We try to discern which prayer-window God may be calling us to open. It is like asking God, "Do you have preference for how we will spend this time together today?" Our resistance is one of the surest guides in discerning a life-giving direction in which to begin a prayer time. For example, we may be troubled by a disturbance in our relationship with another person. Our inclination may be to resist looking at it, and instead to turn away from it and escape to a time of calm and peaceful prayer. If we do, it is likely to plague us as a "distraction" and we will have anything but a peaceful prayer time. The very disturbance itself is an indication of life and movement. We are more likely to find life by centering on the disturbance, welcoming and contemplating the associated feelings or images that surface, and inviting God to be with us in the midst of the chaos or struggle.

One example of such a resistance can be seen in the retreat experience of Michael, a man in his mid-40s. He had chosen to do some drawing with crayons, a new way of prayer for him. When we met, he told me how he had spread the crayons out on the table, closed his eyes and chosen one. It was a dark color and he did not like it. He tried again and got another dark color, which he also rejected. Then he chose some lighter colors, with which he drew the peaceful, happy picture he shared with me. The picture, he said, expressed how he wanted to be, but not how he really was at the time.

Having noticed his resistance to the dark colors, I suggested he draw a picture with them. He did so, and came to our next meeting with a picture that not only expressed more truly who he was at the time, but brought to his mind a painful memory from his childhood. His picture expressed the darkness and turmoil of the memory; it also included a bright and hopeful light to guide him to wholeness and healing. He continued to draw with the crayons and to respond to the challenge being presented to him. By a roundabout and surprising way, he came to a clear and confident decision about a major choice he needed to make in his life.

A moment of trust in his inner Self occurred for Michael when he consciously and courageously chose to pick up the dark, rejected crayons and to let the Spirit speak to him through them. The Spirit led him in what I have come to recognize as a characteristically indirect way. The initial memory that arose for healing had no obvious, conscious connection with the major decision Michael needed to make. Yet out of the process of courageously facing and contemplating the painful memory, there came a healing of the memory, and a new wisdom and confidence that he could bring to any life situation. He could discern the direction of the same Spirit guiding him in a different situation. His choice became clear and simple, and he felt a new confidence to act on it.

Another common experience of resistance arises when we remember a dream we would rather forget, perhaps a nightmare we cannot put out of our mind. One such nightmare is the frightening and disgusting dream I recounted in Chapter Two, in which a man cut off my hands. If we would like to explore a dream during prayer and have several to choose from, the most life-giving and healing dream is invariably the one we resist. The nightmare is like a gold mine: If we go down into its dark depths we most likely will discover a precious treasure.

Aside from the obvious resistance surfacing in these two examples, discernment at the beginning of prayer is normally a much more subtle process. Often we begin a prayer time with several issues, no one of which seems to stand out. We might ask our body to choose one of the situations with which we are currently concerned. We can set them in front of ourselves in our imagination, focus our attention on each one in turn, and notice if our body reacts to any of them. If we notice a reaction to one issue, we might dialogue with our body concerning it.

For example, one such issue I had placed before myself during a particular prayer time was an interview meeting with a prospective new spiritual director scheduled for that afternoon. Consciously, I felt calm about the meeting and was looking forward to it with enthusiasm. However, my stomach tightened up painfully when I focused my attention on the meeting. I asked my stomach what was bothering it. It told me it felt frightened and vulnerable, and was having difficulty digesting the prospect of a new, intimate relationship. I told it I understood, and that it just might continue to feel disturbed until after the meeting and we had a taste of what to expect in this new relationship. It was helpful to know my true feelings before the meeting, as well as to observe how calm my stomach felt after the meeting. I found that I apparently could digest this new relationship after all!

Sometimes our discernment process will reveal an attraction to a particular prayer way with which we are familiar, or perhaps a new way we have not tried before. We discern by paying attention to our own inclinations. Often a very fruitful prayer time will occur when we choose a way that seems as if it will be fun! Our inner child is an excellent companion in prayer, and can lead us with childlike wisdom to a window where our loving God waits for us to come and play awhile. At times we will not experience an inclination toward any particular prayer way. Then we simply need to choose one form of prayer and let our discernment move into the heart of our prayer time, watching and waiting to see what develops in this second area of our consideration.

We practice discernment as we observe the ebb and flow within the particular way of prayer we have chosen.

We look for clues rising from the Spirit within our Self to guide our decisions concerning where to direct our attention as we sit at our chosen prayer-window, as well as whether to move to a different window. Let us look at some concrete examples.

Once during my own retreat, I had decided to go for a walk around the beautiful grounds of the retreat house, meeting God in the stillness and in the beauty of nature. As I walked, I began to feel more and more restless. It occurred to me that my restlessness might be a sign of resistance. I wondered if I needed to look in a direction that was different from the quiet and peace I had chosen. I felt puzzled, however, since nothing on my mind seemed to be of any particular importance. Then an event of the previous day came to mind—an annoying incident that had taken place during the eucharistic liturgy. It hardly seemed worth my attention at this time; it was just a petty annoyance. As I pondered the situation, I realized that the incident had come to mind several times earlier in the day, and I began to suspect that there was more to it than what appeared on the surface. I decided to take a closer look.

As I focused my attention on the incident I found, to my great surprise, that the petty annoyance was but the tip of an iceberg. This seemingly insignificant occurrence was a glimpse of a much larger issue beneath the surface, an issue that was a source of deep pain and anger for me. This raw and open wound needed healing. It became the major focus of my retreat, which was a profoundly healing experience.

The clue of my restlessness led me to a discernment: to take a look around for a different prayer-window than the one I had chosen. It led me to listen for the possibility of the Spirit rattling a window in a different direction. When I followed it, I found a pain far deeper than I suspected— and a loving God who wanted to be with me in my pain and heal my wounded soul.

Another example of resistance and discernment during prayer developed for Susan during her retreat. During one of our first meetings of the retreat, Susan told me she had spent some time in prayer in the chapel, but was troubled with "distractions." She had chosen to sit in simple quiet with God, setting aside her thoughts and feelings for the time. Her stillness was intruded upon by persistent feelings and memories connected with a disturbance in her relationship with a close friend. She had hoped to set aside her struggle with this relationship and have a quiet, restful retreat. She felt a strong resistance to looking at the relationship. The Spirit seemed to have a different agenda. I suggested that she let go of the prayer way she had chosen and center her attention instead on the relationship, contemplating her true feelings about it. She did so, but did not come to any resolution or clarity concerning the relationship.

When we met the next day, Susan shared a dream she remembered from the previous night in which she was in a conflict with a male figure. At first she resisted focusing more closely on the dream man. When she courageously chose to confront the dream figure and try to befriend him, she found a powerful and wise companion. He brought her a gift of heightened clarity and confidence to deal with the relationship with her friend.

She did not solve the conflicts of the relationship during the retreat; those needed to be dealt with in dialogue with her friend. She did leave her retreat with some of the peace she had desired. She felt energized, calm, confident and encouraged with new possibilities to resolve the disturbance—with the help of her new dream friend. Characteristically, the Spirit within her Self was leading her in a roundabout way to an even deeper peace than that which she had been seeking. Her moment of trust in her inner Self came when she chose to let go of her consciously chosen prayer way, overcome her resistance and courageously turn her attention to the chaos of the relationship, looking contemplatively, opening herself to discern the direction of the Spirit there. She was then able to receive the new source of wisdom and strength from within her Self through the gift of her dreams.

Resistance is a consistently reliable signpost pointing in the direction of the Spirit. To discern our own resistance and courageously turn in that direction is one of the most important functions of our ego-self in prayer.

Balance is another reliable sign of the direction of the Spirit—balance among the ways we choose for prayer, balance during prayer, and balance between our inner and outer lives. Let us consider some ways in which balance and resistance can be helpful signs in our discernment of the direction of the Spirit.

One occasion for practicing discernment occurs when our prayer involves strong feelings. Sometimes we may experience emotions so intense that we feel overwhelmed. We need to decide whether to stay with the experience or to move away from it. Balance and resistance can help us discern whether to stay or to leave. In the long run we may simply need to choose, to observe the results and learn by trial and error. We may find that when we choose to stay with an overwhelming feeling in prayer, it tends to remain with us in an intense way and to diminish our ability to function well in our external world. In that case, the need for balance would indicate that a different way of dealing with our feelings may be indicated.

On the other hand, we may find that when we overcome our resistance and courageously allow ourselves to plumb the depths of our emotions in prayer, the feelings become spent. This may free us to see the situation with clearer vision. We may find that the greater our resistance, the more surely the intense experience will lead us toward balance and wholeness in both inner and outer life. In this case, the call to balance would indicate that to turn in the direction of our greatest resistance is to follow the movement of the Spirit.

Dryness in prayer, manifested by sluggishness or boredom, feeling disconnected from God, or feeling lost and wandering, presents an opportunity for discernment. It can have a number of causes. As we attempt to find what is blocking the flow of our prayer, it helps to ask ourselves some questions related to resistance and balance.

For instance, if we have been trying to develop a variety of prayer ways, we might ask if we have been flitting from one prayer window to another and failing to stay long enough at one to allow a contemplative experience to develop. We might be resisting a surfacing feeling by unconsciously moving to another way of prayer, thereby escaping from a difficult issue we need to deal with. In so doing, we can block the movement and flow of the Spirit and thereby experience dryness.

On the other hand, we can also block the flow of prayer by being unwilling to try new prayer ways. We can gradually become accustomed to a form of prayer that has been fruitful for us. We come to expect what our prayer will be like. In the process, we can form an unconscious barrier, a resistance to the surprises God may offer. A new way of prayer can help to provide a more balanced "diet" of prayer ways. It can also help us to break through our own barriers, since we have not had a chance to form expectations.

Developing expectations of any kind in prayer can be deadly; expectations kill the liveliness of prayer by blocking out surprises from God. The only truly realistic expectation for any particular prayer time is that we can make ourselves available. We can set aside a time and take steps to avoid interruptions such as taking the phone off the hook and putting a "do not disturb" sign on the door.

In the long run it is realistic to expect prayer to be fruitful and nourishing, since God's desire for intimacy with us is far greater than any desire of ours. God passionately wants to come ever closer to us. If we experience dryness in prayer for a time, it is wise to look first for ways we may be resisting, and to ask God to reveal any barrier that is blocking us. Then when we have done all we can to uncover and move past our own resistance, often all we can do is wait. Imagine what this is like: perhaps a desert, perhaps a brick wall, perhaps a child lost and wandering in a dense forest. We can center our attention and contemplate the desert or the wall or the forest. Our very helplessness can remind us that we don't encounter God in prayer by our own efforts. Remember in times of dryness that ours is a good and gracious God who loves to surprise us when we least expect it, and who in time will break through even our unconscious barriers. For our part, we need only to make ourselves available, to remain open and willing to receive the Spirit.

The third area of discernment begins at that point of transition in prayer where we sense that it is time to move outward and begin to integrate our prayer experience into our total life. We can discern the ways our inner experience fits into place in our outer life. We can allow it to influence the decisions we make concerning our actions. We can open ourselves to the creative energy, courage and clarity our prayer experience may bring to our outer life.

Let us look at how balance and resistance can be used in our discernment during the integration process. Consider the situation where we find it difficult to shift our attention to our external life. Perhaps our prayer experience has been a particularly compelling or powerful one, and we resist shifting our attention to the seemingly mundane activities of daily life. We need to look at the balance, at the appropriate place of prayer in the context of our total experience. An example from my own experience will illustrate this balance between inner and outer reality.

A few years ago, for a period of several weeks, my prayer was punctuated by some powerful and awesome spir-

itual experiences. I felt very close to God. I was amazed
and overwhelmed by the intensity of the experiences, which
tended to occur at the end of the time I had set aside for
prayer. I had read in several different books on prayer that
one hour should be the limit for a single prayer period, so
I stopped after an hour. However, it seemed that God would
not really want me to leave at a time when we were so close.
I was confused, and discussed the matter with my spiritual
director at our next meeting. I expected him to say that in
the midst of such a powerful experience, it was all right to
lengthen my prayer time. I was surprised when he said it
was best to stop at the end of an hour, and that both Ignatius
of Loyola and Teresa of Avila recommended an hour limit.

After I left the meeting with my spiritual director, I
felt a sense of childlike pouting and rebellion. I resisted
looking at these feelings at first. I did not want to admit,
even to myself, that I could have such an immature attitude.
After a while, however, I realized that my inner child was
clamoring for some attention, so I decided to set aside my
resistance and to get in touch with her. As I played the role
of "little Jeannie," I found that I was indeed pouting. I found
it hard to accept the advice of my spiritual director. I decided to go over his head and take it up with God.

The next day, I went to God in prayer as the loving
Father I had come to know and to feel very close to. I felt
like a tattletale as I crawled into his lap and let him put his
arm around me. He listened attentively as I complained
that "all three of them are ganging up on me—my spiritual
director, Ignatius, and Teresa!" I said it was like giving me
a big ice cream sundae with three different flavors of ice
cream and syrup—topped off with a big mound of whipped
cream and a cherry—and then taking it away from me after
I had taken one bite! When I had finished tattling and com-
plaining, I was ready to listen to what he had to say in
response. His answer is as powerful today as it was then.
He drew me closer to himself and said in the most tender

and loving voice imaginable: "My child, you only need a taste. If you eat the whole thing, you'll get fat!"

My anger and rebelliousness evaporated instantly as I laughed aloud at his reply. I accepted his answer easily. "Little Jeannie" was satisfied. As I pondered the experience, I came to see clearly that to stay longer than an hour in prayer was to limit my experience of God. It would be out of balance. These joyous and powerful experiences of God were but one face of God. I needed to turn to my everyday life and allow God's other faces to be revealed to me in the faces of my family and friends and other people I encountered in my daily life, in the shopping and the laundry and the cooking, in the wonders of nature and all the dimensions of my life. I needed a balanced diet of God—not just dessert!

Our inner and outer experience needs to be in balance. The time we set aside for prayer needs to be in harmony with our way of life. It is not an escape from life, but a time for nourishment and light—a time to connect our outer life with the inner resources of the Spirit within our Self, that we might live all of our life more fully and authentically.

If we discern that we are out of balance toward inner reality—if we feel a resistance to finding God's face in outer reality—we can take steps to bring about a more centered posture. One effective technique is to express the inner experience in a concrete outer way such as writing or drawing. This activity honors both inner and outer worlds, helps to get it off our mind and onto the paper, channels or directs the inner spiritual power outward and helps us carry the experience more lightly as we move about in the outer world. We no longer need to be weighed down by keeping our treasured prayer experience with us every moment, afraid we will lose it if we do not carry it constantly on our mind. We can see it in tangible form on paper, and so our fear of losing it is calmed and we are better able to go about our business.

One such powerful experience for me was the Igor Stravinsky/volcano story I described in Chapter Two. I decided to draw a large picture illustrating the experience. I portrayed four of the scenes in separate frames, two at each end of the picture. The center was the fifth and climactic scene in which I shot out of the volcano into the arms of God as Mother and Father. I depicted the lava coming up from a channel whose source is at the center of the earth. It goes so deep that it is far below my consciousness, out of sight and off the bottom of the picture. The image comes into my memory from time to time. When it does, I typically feel a deep calm and sense of God's life-giving presence: the power of the Spirit flowing from the very center of my being like the steady flow of the lava from the center of the earth. The experience at first felt overpowering, with a tendency to pull me out of balance toward my inner world. Drawing the picture enabled me to contain and channel the energy into my outer experience in a steady, balanced way.

Sometimes we may feel an urge to integrate our inner experience by seeing a specific meaning or connection with our outer life situation. This can give rise to another kind of resistance and imbalance. Suppose, for example, that our prayer experience has been very interesting and moving, but puzzling. We do not find any specific connection with anything in our life, or we see only a vague and indefinite meaning. We sense a meaning beyond our grasp. So we begin to grasp for the meaning. We work on it, analyze it, but it eludes us. Perhaps we begin to feel tired or get a headache. The feeling may be like grabbing and holding on. The imbalance here is found in the draining of energy as we try to get hold of the meaning, especially when we begin to realize that we are making very little progress. We can begin to discern the imbalance in the feeling of working at it, as opposed to toying with it or playing with it. We discern resistance in our analytical approach, which we can consciously control. Our ego-self works and holds on, resisting the surprising way our inner Self may connect with our

external life, perhaps in a way we are reluctant or unable
to see.

The discernment process is subtle, and requires a contemplative attitude that enables us to listen for the still,
small voice of the Spirit whispering to us in and through our
prayer experiences and our entire life. No matter what form
of prayer we use, there is opportunity for our ego-self to
hold on and control, as well as to let go. For example, if we
are praying outside in the natural world we may simply
sense a deep connection with the life of the Creator, feeling
nurtured and rejuvenated. Then our ego-self may try to
control by analyzing the experience—seeking to see how a
certain situation is like the river or the tree, for instance—
then trying to see how we need to change ourselves, rather
than letting our Creator change us in ways we cannot see.
Somewhere in the process it begins to feel like work—and
that is a good sign that we are holding on with our ego-self,
"playing God"—and that we need to let go and let God do
God's work.

In order to channel the flow of spiritual life and power
from our prayer into the whole of our life, we need to carry
our prayer experiences lightly and hold them loosely, so that
we do not constrict the flow. Then our discernment can
become contemplative in the context of our life, and the
meaning will emerge in time. It will simply flow into the
proper place in our life if we carry it gently. In fact, it may
happen so gently that we do not even notice it until we
realize we have changed in some way, perhaps feeling more
balanced or whole, deeply peaceful or grateful, stronger or
more authentic, more loving and accepting of ourselves and
others. In other words, we come to look more and more
like Jesus in the gospels, the primary sign that we are moving in the direction of the Spirit of God.

Notice how often the phrase *practicing discernment in
prayer* has been used in this chapter. The period of time
we set aside for prayer might well be seen as a time to

practice discerning the movement and direction of the Spirit—with the goal of learning to discern the movement and direction of the Spirit at all times, throughout our daily lives. We might compare it to learning to play the piano. We may spend years increasing our skill as well as our feel for the music. It is a lot of work at first, and we need to concentrate on such details as reading the music and the placement of our fingers on the keyboard. After a time those details become automatic and we no longer need to concentrate our attention on them. We begin to enjoy the music more, and our own distinctive style begins to emerge. Our playing progressively expresses our unique feelings and moods. Those skills and techniques over which we labored during our many practice times in the early years have become a part of ourselves, no longer needing our conscious attention. Now our attention can be focused on the whole of the music. In a sense the music becomes an extension of ourselves, an expression of who we are at the moment. We become one with the music.

Likewise, as we practice discernment in prayer periods we learn skills that in time become part of ourselves. We do not need to consciously pay attention to learning techniques. We become more contemplative, increasingly able to discern the movement and direction of the Spirit in all of our life. We find it more and more natural to incorporate our prayerful discernment into our everyday life. The limits of our prayer period are broken as we begin to notice inner movements outside of our prayer time, movements that we previously were able to discern only within the stillness of our prayer period. Those limits blur as we grow more and more consistently in touch with the Spirit within our Self. Our contemplative experience expands beyond the boundaries of our prayer period into all of our life. In a very real sense, prayer expands to all of life; we become one with prayer, one with life, one with God. The prayer-windows that we had been opening one at a time during our prayer

periods are all open now, all of the time. We are open to
the gentle breezes and the stormy winds of the Spirit from
all directions in the whole of our lives.

The process of discernment is subtle and shadowy, and
we can easily become lost in the tangled growth and inter-
woven paths of the spiritual journey. It can be extremely
helpful to walk with a companion and guide who is familiar
with the terrain of the inner world: a spiritual director. In
spiritual direction, our companion looks with us at our spiritual experience in the context of our life. Together, we
attempt to discern the direction of the Spirit.

In sharing our spiritual experience with another person
who listens and receives our gift with reverence and care,
we can develop a growing trust in our own inner experience.
Involving another person in the discernment process also
adds an element of objectivity. It is difficult to uncover our
own resistance, which is usually unconscious. We are often
unaware of imbalance in our lives. We are simply too close;
spiritual experience is highly subjective. The affirmation of
our spiritual experience, objectivity in discernment, and
encouragement in overcoming resistance are gifts that can
be ours when we decide to entrust the story of our spiritual
journey to our companion.

The choice of a spiritual director is itself a process of
discernment. It is important to arrange an interview with
anyone you are considering as a possible spiritual director.
Besides being an opportunity to discover whether or not
you can relate well with the prospective director, the interview can be a time to explore whether or not the two of you
have a compatible view of your expectations of the direction
process. It is also a time to ask practical questions such as
the length and frequency of meetings—normally about an
hour, once a month or perhaps more frequently for the first
few meetings. Another practical question to ask concerns
any donation or fee that may be expected. It would probably
be helpful for the prospective director to know something

of your living and working situations, the significant relationships in your life, the ways you pray regularly, and any previous experiences of spiritual direction.

End an initial interview with no strings attached for either person—no appointment made to meet again and no commitment to contact the director with your decision. This leaves you very free to make a choice without the pressure of feeling a responsibility to tell a prospective director that you have chosen someone else. Also, remember that the interview is two-way. The choice needs to be mutual, with both you and the director agreeing to enter into this very significant relationship.

After the interview, take at least one or two days to consider the possibility of direction with this person, even if it seemed very positive during the interview. Allow yourself time to bring the question to prayer and to observe your inner movements whenever the issue comes to mind. It can be very helpful to sleep on it, literally asking for a dream to help shed light on the question.

The discernment process can continue even after direction begins. Sometimes the choice does not become clear until after a few meetings. For this reason, it may help to agree to evaluate the relationship after a specific number of meetings. Both of you can look at how it is for you. The evaluation can either affirm the choice or perhaps indicate that something different is in order. For instance, it may become clear that spiritual direction is not really appropriate at this particular time. Instead, perhaps pastoral counseling is called for to address a specific issue, or psychotherapy to deal with an especially intense situation. In a long-term spiritual direction relationship it can be helpful to have an evaluation periodically, perhaps every six months or so.

Our consideration of discernment and direction would lack an essential element without a look at one of the most common barriers to be encountered along the spiritual journey, perhaps the only real barrier, the one that underlies

all of our resistance. From time to time along our journey
we all encounter an inability to believe in and to receive the
incredibly tender, passionate and unconditional love of God
for each one of us individually. We might ask ourselves how
it could be so hard to allow ourselves to be loved by God.
How could we resist what would seem to be such an obviously joyous experience?

One facet of our resistance to God's love for us is a fear
of "God's will" that we may experience from time to time.
It may seem that God's will for us is somehow separate from
our own will, that God may want something for us that will
not make us happy. We are afraid to trust God completely.
The distortion in this concept of God becomes clear when
it is placed alongside the image of God as portrayed by
Jesus, an all-loving God who always wants to lead us toward
healing, happiness and wholeness. Just as God's image is
clearly reflected in the image of our Self, God's will is clearly
reflected in the will of our deeper Self as we discern what
we truly want.

This fear of God is a subtle barrier, powerful and difficult to discern. Our resistance to God's love is like clay in
the hands of a sculptor. Imagine yourself as a sculptor mold-
ing a work of art from a piece of clay. You enjoy the process.
The clay is soft and resistant at the same time. It yields to
your touch, yet it has its own inherent texture and limitations. You need to respect the essential qualities of the clay.
You are in touch with the clay in a way you couldn't be in
working, for instance, with marble. Your hands become
coated with the clay as you work. You begin to feel like a
partner with the clay as you shape it and discover its possibilities as well as its limitations. You learn about each other
in the sculpturing process. You tell the clay what you want
it to become and it answers by yielding to your touch at one
time and, at another, surprising you with its inability to be
shaped as you intend.

As you work, you see little cracks and bumps but you

take little note of them. You know it is all part of the for-
mation process. These apparent flaws will disappear and be
incorporated into the shape, and then new bumps and cracks
will appear as the shape is further developed. None of that
matters, though. You are engrossed in the process of the
shaping. You feel delighted as the shape you had in mind
begins to emerge—and delighted also when a part of the
shape surprises you. The clay seems to have an idea of what
it would like to become. You are pleased with the process
and with the emerging shape. You feel more and more one
with the clay, as if you and the clay are intimately involved
in the creative process together.

Now imagine that you are the clay. At first, you like
the touch of the sculptor. You like the attention. It feels like
a loving touch. You like the shape you are becoming. It feels
good to be soft and let yourself be shaped. It is fun to see
how creative the sculptor is, what surprising shapes emerge.
Then you notice a few cracks and bumps. You begin to doubt
the skill of the sculptor. How can you become a beautiful
and lovable work of art with these ugly flaws? You become
stiffer, resisting the sculptor's touch. You do not want to be
full of flaws. Your joy begins to fade.

Then you decide to take a chance and see what this
sculptor will do with the cracks and bumps. You become
soft again and absorbed in the shape you are becoming. The
joy begins to return. You forget about the flaws for a while
in your joy at the surprising and interesting new shape.
When you look again, the flaws you saw before are gone,
but there are new ones in different places. You begin to
suspect that these rough spots are part of the process. Maybe
it will be all right to let them be, to let the sculptor deal
with them, to incorporate them into the emerging form.

Now you are not so sure you like the shape that is
emerging. You want to be a little different shape. You become hard and stiff in some places, softer in others, trying
to influence the shape. You succeed. Then you look at the

resulting form. It seems to have lost some of the grace and beauty that it had previously. So you become soft again. Again, you allow the sculptor to have a hand in your shaping. You are surprised and delighted that the somewhat clumsy lines that you influenced are now incorporated into the emerging shape in an exciting new way under the touch of the sculptor's hand. You begin to feel the love and the joy of the sculptor. You begin to trust again, deeper this time. You feel one with the sculptor, partners in your own creation. You are more willing to stay soft, and to welcome the sculptor's touch.

Our resistance is inherent in our human nature, an essential quality of our clay-ness. When we experience resistance, we are feeling God's touch. It is a sign of life in our relationship with God. We know God is very close, inviting us to be partners in a new shaping, a new step in the ongoing process of our creation. Our resistance is a natural hesitation. Perhaps we are afraid of looking at the flaws that we know will be part of the process, remembering how ugly they seemed before. Perhaps we are unwilling at the moment to let go of our control of the shape we will take, afraid we will not like the shape into which God will form us. Maybe we are afraid that a new shape will uncover gifts and abilities that will bring with them a responsibility· to exercise them and to share them with others.

Perhaps, having tasted the awesome and wondrous power of the Sculptor's hands, at the very core of our being we are terrified that we will be squashed into a mere lump, losing our identity or even being obliterated into nothingness. This very real fear, though largely unconscious, underlies much of our resistance. We overcome our resistance and summon up the courage to yield to God's touch when we remember the love and tenderness we have felt before, the beauty God has created in us previously. When we simply decide to trust again, courageously making that choice, we open ourselves to the new beauty and grace and freedom that God wants to create in us. We learn again that our good and gracious God wants us to be happy and free, and acts always and only for our good. Our belief grows deeper, our courage grows stronger and we can freely choose, again and again, to open ourselves to the loving, tender, powerful, awesome, creative touch of the Master Sculptor.

SEVEN

The Return of the Kangaroo

As I was writing the early part of this book, the kangaroo image returned to me in a new dream. She has accompanied me throughout the writing process. The story is a rich expression of my own journey in prayer, and has much to say about prayer in general.

In my dream, I am vacationing in a cabin with my family and another family. There are several children from both families there, perhaps six or seven. I had found a tiny kangaroo with soft gray fur, and had brought her into the cabin and hidden her in a drawer in the kitchen. I seem to be reluctant to let her out for fear the other adults will disapprove and not want me to keep her. However, I realize she has been in the drawer for several days, and I have forgotten to get her out and care for her. I am worried that she is dead by now, or almost dead, from lack of food and water. I am upstairs in the bedroom when I remember the little kangaroo again. I am ashamed that I have still not taken care of her, and even more worried that she may be dead. I write a note to remind myself to take her out as soon as I go downstairs, but again I forget.

Later, as I am coming down the stairs again and into the kitchen, I realize that the children have discovered the little kangaroo. They have taken her out of the drawer and given her some food and water. She has recovered from her neglect and is hopping around the kitchen, full of pep and as lively as when I had found her. No one seems to object to her, as I had feared. She fits right in with the group and has joined in the fun. I am delighted to see her, and greatly relieved that she is alive and well.

I pick up the little kangaroo and hold her in my hands, close to my face. My heart softens with affection for this lovable little animal. I tell her how sorry I am that I forgot her for so long, and how happy I am that she is all right. She rubs her head against my cheek in a gesture of tender love and forgiveness. She feels cuddly and warm, and I love the soft, gray color of her fur. It is a profoundly intimate moment, full of warmth and affection.

The scene shifts, and I am preparing a simple breakfast for several of the adults who have not yet eaten. A young, blond-haired boy, about 8 or 9 years old, is helping me.

After awakening from the dream, I felt a joy and delight that returned numerous times throughout the day, whenever I remembered the dream and the lovable little kangaroo. I was repeatedly amazed every time I realized that I had really dreamt of a kangaroo. The return of the image, especially in this delightful miniature form, was a mysterious and wondrous gift to me.

I returned to the dream in my imagination in prayer the next day and numerous other times since then. I wanted to get to know this tiny kangaroo better. I found that her name was Katie. I talked with the boy who had helped me with breakfast. He introduced himself as Mike. As I had guessed, he was one of the children who had found Katie and cared for her. I thanked Mike for what he had done for her. I told him I was worried that Katie would get stepped on or lost, because she was so small. He suggested that we make a cage for her, so she would be safe when we could not watch her. I thought it was a good idea, so we made the cage, even though I began to feel that it might not be a good thing to do after all.

After a time, I realized I felt caged in prayer. I did not know why or how I felt inhibited, but only sensed a barrier. I decided it truly was a bad idea to cage Katie. However, before I could set her free, I needed to overcome my fear that she might be lost or killed. At first I could not do it. I compromised by giving Katie a key to the cage so she could let herself out when she wanted to, but could also be protected if necessary. After a while, still feeling restrained in prayer, I tearfully brought my anguish to Katie. As I told her of my desire to be freer and more in touch with God, she suddenly grew as large as Maggie, the orange kangaroo from my childhood. She simply outgrew the cage! It was now obsolete.

Katie's soft gray color reminds me of the gentle gray doves of my childhood, which in turn remind me of the soft, whispering voice of the Spirit within my Self. I sense that my desire for contemplative prayer was born during the quiet times in the back yard of my childhood home. Maggie seems to have returned from my memory to reawaken that hunger for God in prayer. Maggie's orange color seems so expressive of the vivid, definite, unmistakable movements of God in my life. Katie's soft gray color reminds me of the gentler, quieter movements of the Spirit within my Self.

Katie seems to have come to transform my prayer further, to help me to let go of boundaries I have subtly formed, caging my prayer as most of us do from time to time. For instance, I had become so accustomed to vivid and dramatic imagery in my prayer that I could miss the calmer, more subtle movements of the Spirit. Katie's gray color also suggests no definite boundaries, no black and white, but rather a blending into the total landscape. The boundaries of my prayer time have become blurred, blending into my total life experience as I notice with increasing frequency the movements of the Spirit as they occur throughout the entire day and night.

I found it interesting that a fear of the other adults motivated me to hide Katie away in the drawer and inhibited me from letting her run free. I seemed to think they would have some rules about what kind of animals, if any, would be allowed in the cabin. It reminds me of the "shoulds" regarding prayer that I discover in myself from time to time. Rules for the way prayer should be keep me from letting the Spirit lead me to new ways to be with God. The children, who paid no attention to such imaginary rules, simply let Katie out! My own inner children often do the same for me.

Katie has enticed me beyond the upstairs place of my special time of prayer and into the kitchen—the place of nourishment, the gathering place for family and friends— the hub of my everyday life. She came into a vacation place, reminding me that prayer is not work but more like spending time with God in a relaxed and intimate way. Katie is a wonderful companion, bringing her playfulness when I begin to take my self too seriously, carrying me in her pouch when I am lost or when I am afraid to explore new territory, fiercely protecting me if I feel endangered.

Maggie and Katie have shown me many new paths that lead to the Spirit deep within my unconscious Self. These two wondrous creatures from "The Land Down Under" seem to know their way around my subconscious Self very well! They both continue to reveal new shapes and colors of God to me. They are awesome, joyous, powerful, adorable, playful, lovable, wise and challenging—just like God.

Maggie, Katie and I invite you to trust your Self . . .
    to look, to touch, to discover, to welcome . . .
        to open all of your prayer windows . . .
    to let the Spirit blow freely
        from deep within your Self . . .
    to let in God's love in a kaleidoscope of colors . . .
        to throw away your boundaries and cages . . .
    to let yourself be shaped into the shape of God . . .
        your own unique shape . . .
            lovable . . . precious . . . graceful . . .
            full of life and wonder . . . full of God . . .
    and then to sing an Alleluia of praise . . .
        that you are so beautifully, wonderfully made.

MY PSALM

An Epilogue

I lift my thankful heart to you, my God; I sing your praise.
  I shout from the highest mountain;
    I leap toward the stars.
You have done wondrous things to me,
  and holy is your name.
You have taken my heart of stone
  and given me a heart of flesh.
I give my heart to you;
  I pour out my life in your praise.

I have hung my head in shame, afraid to look at your face;
  my tears fell to the ground, my body racked with sobs.
You tenderly cupped my chin in your hand
  and lifted my face to look upon your countenance.
    And I was filled with your love for me.
You kissed away my tears,
  and held me in your arms
    until my sobbing ceased.

You have lifted me up
   and touched my face with your hand;
     you healed my broken heart.
You have looked upon me with love;
   you have touched me and made me whole.
How wondrous are your works, O Lord;
   you knit me in my mother's womb.
I give thanks to you, my good and gracious God,
   for I am fearfully, wonderfully made.

I have walked through the flames of death,
   and your hand has shielded me from harm.
I have fallen into the deep pit,
   and you have lifted me up with your right hand.

My heart sings your praise, O Lord,
   and my spirit rejoices.
I would climb the highest mountain,
   search the darkest valley,
   sail to the edge of the sea,
   fly to the farthest star
      to touch your hand, my God,
      to look upon your face,
      to be lost in your embrace.

I have been lost in my grief, O my God,
   searching like a lost child,
   wandering in the deep, dark forest of my soul.
I called out to you,
   and you did not answer.
I cried, "How long, O Lord, how long?
   How long must I wander,
     with only my tears to quench my thirst,
     with only my empty heart to comfort me?"
And you came like a stag,
   leaping through the tangled thicket,
     sure-footed and strong.
You carried me on your back

when my strength was gone.
You refreshed me and brought me back to life.
You led me out of darkness
    into your own wonderful light.
You caressed my body
    and made me holy.
You cast my enemies to the ground,
    and brought me back to yourself.
My God, how I thirst for you.
    My body longs for your touch;
        my soul yearns for you unceasingly.
How I long to be in your presence,
    lost in your embrace,
        never to be parted from you again.

I dance in praise and thanksgiving to you, O my God.
    I twirl and swirl and spin with joy;
    I bow down before your face;
    I prostrate myself in wonder and awe
        at your feet, my Lord and my God.

My good and gracious God, how wondrous are your works,
    how delightful are your creatures.
How the stars and the moon proclaim your majesty;
    the rivers and streams sing your name;
    the trees sway in the wind,
        dancing with joy and thanksgiving.
Would that I could sing and dance
    with music that could reach the heavens,
        and harmonize with your great love, my God.
Yet my heart feels as if it will burst,
    throbbing with love for you, my Lord.
Hold my heart in your hands, my Lover,
    where it will burst and I will be destroyed,
        lost in your depths,
            swallowed in your embrace,
    no more myself, but one with you.

I tremble before you, my God.
>I fear your touch;
>>I long for your embrace.
Where can I go, my God,
>but to run into your arms?
If I turn and flee, you are there.
>If I fly like an eagle,
>>soaring to the highest heights,
>>>I fly into your arms.
>If I sink into the darkest depths,
>>I find myself in the dark warmth of your womb,
>>filled with your life,
>>>secure in your warmth.
Then I am brought to birth again,
>received as a helpless babe into your arms,
>filled with the sweet, warm milk of your breast,
>slumbering in peace against your soft, warm breast.
What can I say, my God?
>I have no more words,
>>no more music,
>>>no more images of you.
I long to sink into silence,
>the deep silence of you,
>>the abyss, the darkness where you are.
I long to be lost in you, O my God,
>my Love, my Mother, my Father,
>>my Joy, my Hope, my All.
>>>>Amen.

>>>>>Alleluia!